Rhetoric and Storytelling within the U.S. Asylum Process

This book explores the U.S. asylum process and how those seeking shelter deal with the rhetorical pressures of compelling asylum narratives they need to write in order to stay.

Centered around a study conducted at a shelter on the U.S. border, this book moves beyond this context to demonstrate how liminal sites provide opportunities for displaced communities to employ distinct shared rhetorical practices of daily life—like silence and routine—that both safeguard vulnerabilities and enact agency for individuals within precarious spaces. Placing people who seek asylum and those who work with them as rhetorical and sociocultural experts on this issue, the study adds to the emerging importance of rhetoric within discussions of asylum and forced migration and demonstrates the significance of rhetorical ecology theory as part of a blended methodology in understanding people seeking asylum as a group in a perpetual and explicit state of ethos development.

Highlighting the need for support which is sensitive to the narrative struggles people seeking asylum face, this book will have important findings for scholars and upper-level students of cultural rhetorics, feminist rhetoric, migration studies, political science, and intercultural communication.

Mónica Reyes is Assistant Professor in the Writing, Rhetoric & Discourse Department at DePaul University. Her research interests include cultural rhetorics; rhetorical ecologies; critical refugee studies; and transnational feminist rhetorical literacies. Her work has been featured most recently in *Grassroots Activisms: Public Rhetorics in Localized Contexts* (2024); *Enculturation: A Journal of Rhetoric, Writing & Culture* (2020); and *Postcolonial Text* (2019). She is also a Public Voices Fellow of The OpEd Project.

Routledge Studies in Rhetoric and Communication

41 **American Women Activists and Autobiography**
Rhetorical Lives
Heather Ostman

42 **Language and Power on the Rhetorical Stage: Theory in the Body**
Fiona Harris Ramsby

43 **Violence, Silence, and Rhetorical Cultures of Champion-Building in Sports**
Kathleen Sandell Hardesty

44 **Difficult Empathy and Rhetorical Encounters**
Eric Leake

45 **Patients Making Meaning**
Theorizing Sources of Information and Forms of Support in Women's Health
Bryna Siegel Finer, Cathryn Molloy and Jamie Farnham

46 **Evangelical Writing in a Secular Imaginary**
The Academic Writing of Christian Undergraduates at a Public University
Emily Murphy Cope

47 **Children as Rhetorical Advocates in Social Movements**
Luke Winslow and Eli Mangold

48 **Rhetoric and Storytelling within the U.S. Asylum Process**
Shelter Rhetorics
Mónica Reyes

Rhetoric and Storytelling within the U.S. Asylum Process

Shelter Rhetorics

Mónica Reyes

NEW YORK AND LONDON

First published 2025
by Routledge
605 Third Avenue, New York, NY 10158

and by Routledge
4 Park Square, Milton Park, Abingdon, Oxon, OX14 4RN

Routledge is an imprint of the Taylor & Francis Group, an informa business

ISBN: 978-1-032-38285-2 (hbk)
ISBN: 978-1-032-39430-5 (pbk)
ISBN: 978-1-003-34969-3 (ebk)

DOI: 10.4324/9781003349693

Typeset in Times New Roman
by KnowledgeWorks Global Ltd.

For Carmen

Contents

Figures

Abbreviations

CBP Customs and Border Protection
ELL English Language Learning
LPP La Posada Providencia
RGV Rio Grande Valley
UNHCR United Nations High Commission on Refugees
UTRGV The University of Texas Rio Grande Valley

1 A Short Tour of the Project

I'll always remember Blanca, an elderly woman with diminishing eyesight who I met while volunteering at an emergency shelter for displaced people in my native community in the Rio Grande Valley of south Texas. Blanca had fled her country because she and her son had faced death threats from a local gang that operated with law enforcement. Her son had arrived in the U.S. before she did while she traveled with a group that arrived in Brownsville, Texas. Blanca seemed frail and needed help walking; because of her health, I was surprised she was able to make the trip.

She had been at the shelter for a week, and that morning, the case manager had arranged for me to help Blanca begin to tell her story about why she left her country to help get her asylum process going. Blanca was glad for the help, and after I introduced myself, she explained to me that she didn't know she would have to tell her story in such detail about why she left. She thought it was obvious to people in the U.S. that such dangers existed every day in her country. She then admitted that she didn't know how to read or write, and she felt overwhelmed.

As Blanca and I talked, she decided that she wasn't ready to share, as her story was much too traumatic for her to relive. She was tired, and she just wanted to see her son. We decided to spend time looking at the gardens on the property instead, and she shared her extensive knowledge about gardening with me. Within a week, Blanca had moved on; she connected with pro-bono legal resources, began her application, and was on her way to see her son with help from the shelter team.

Blanca represents one of 70 million displaced people globally, including over 3 million people seeking asylum (UNHCR). Over half of those seeking asylum in the U.S. enter through the ports of entry within my native community, the Rio Grande Valley (RGV). Of the 54,690 people apprehended on the U.S. border who claimed credible fear in 2018 (the last year data was available), 32,521 entered through the RGV ("U.S. Border Patrol Claims of Credible Fear Apprehensions by Sector").

Through my steady volunteer work at the shelter, I became curious about how people seeking asylum status, like Blanca, may come to realize that

DOI: 10.4324/9781003349693-1

their own stories are the most powerful resource that they have. For people who have been displaced, stories of persecution allow them to build "credible" fear-based accounts that allow them to begin their asylum process in the U.S. In fact, the United States Citizenship & Immigration Services (the official U.S. government body that adjudicates claims) outline that a person is eligible to apply for asylum if they are able to effectively persuade the U.S. government (in writing) that they are "unable or unwilling to return to his or her country of nationality … because of persecution or a well-founded fear of persecution on account of race, religion, nationality, membership in a particular social group, or political opinion" ("Application for Asylum" 2). I came to understand that the stories required by the U.S. asylum process are underpinned with ideological complications and contradictions; not only are people who seek asylum at the national border blanketly criminalized, but they are also simultaneously required to tell stories which homogenize them as victims in order to be considered credible. Either as a criminal or victim (or a troubling combination of both), there is an underlying ideology at work which positions the nation-state as the exclusive means to agency and belonging.

However, displaced people, like all humans, tell a variety of stories, which often resist hegemonic narratives about asylum-seeking experiences, and these stories can be just as powerful in helping them live their lives along their journey. For example, Blanca had been victimized, separated from her family, and experienced emotional and physical turmoil. She also lacked reading and writing skills that would allow her to complete an asylum application on her own. However, Blanca also demonstrated agency by choosing to collaborate with someone to help share her story. Later, when Blanca decided that storytelling would retraumatize her, she made the decision to exercise silence about those experiences to protect herself. She pivoted to topics (gardening) and stories that didn't focus on her as a displaced person even though she had left behind the only home she'd ever known.

Blanca's rhetorics of displacement indicate how the variety of stories displaced people tell about themselves are influenced by their rhetorical ecology—a varied and shifting context of narratives, events, people, materials, and policies—that is the U.S. asylum system. For example, someone who recently arrived and is seeking asylum may attempt to compose their story within a space like a border patrol holding cell, detention center, or shelter. Each of these spaces has its own unique staff, as well as approach and goal for listening to stories, making the process of storytelling challenging for people seeking asylum to navigate.

In this book, I examine La Posada Providencia (LPP) as a case study. I argue that LPP operates as an influential "Third Space" for asylum hopefuls as evidenced through distinct shared rhetorical practices of daily life that both safeguard vulnerabilities and enact agency for individuals within precarious spaces, what I term *shelter rhetorics*. To better interpret their quotidian experience, I conducted audio-recorded interviews and invited the LPP community to create visualizations (drawings and photos). Third Space, as articulated by respective Chicana feminists such as Candace Zepeda, Lisa A. Flores, and Adela C. Licona, posits that in-between sites, such as LPP, may provide space for marginalized people to cultivate alternative perspectives and shared rhetorical practices which speak back to hegemonic and fixed representations of their experiences. Ultimately, I argue how people who seek asylum and those who work with them within liminal spaces like shelters are able to operate among the transnational ideological tensions of asylum through collaboratively building a Third Space where they are able to critique overlapping discourses of social identity, agency, and kinship through shared cross-cultural rhetorics of daily life.

This work is highly interdisciplinary; thus, I used a blend of methodological lenses derived from cultural rhetorics, rhetorical ecologies, and Chicana feminisms; it was also necessary to borrow from the field of refugee and forced migration studies throughout the project. Such a blended methodology not only calls attention to the complexity of the asylum process and the individuals who must endure it but also demonstrates the layered approach required to listen to people about their lived experiences. A few pivotal questions helped shape the research: (1) How does LPP operate as a rhetorical network within the rhetorical ecology of the U.S. asylum system? (2) How does the shelter, as a networked site, afford or constrain the variety of stories people seeking asylum tell about their lived experiences? (3) How do the stories produced at the shelter perpetuate or critique the hegemonic narratives of asylum circulating within the rhetorical ecology of the U.S. asylum system?

Instead of focusing on the travel narratives of clients, which may have seriously risked perpetuating victim stereotypes and traumatic narrative fetishes, this book foregrounds the quotidian or "dailyness" of life at LPP. By giving room to the everyday, seemingly inconsequential practices which make up people's lives, this book reveals larger perspectives or ideological alignments (De Certeau; The Cultural Rhetorics Theory Lab) about how displaced people tell stories on their own terms.

La Posada Providencia

LPP is classified as an "emergency shelter for immigrants, asylum seekers and asylees recently processed by U.S. immigration authorities" and provides complete care (shelter, meals, conversational English classes, case management) for up to 25 displaced individuals (men, women, and families) at a time. Started in 1989 by a community of Roman Catholic Sisters, the shelter was initially created as a material response to the need for a temporary refuge for impoverished immigrants, asylees, and people seeking asylum in the RGV of south Texas.

It wasn't until 2017 that LPP hired an executive director to oversee the shelter's operations in tandem with the three Sisters who live on-site. Additionally, there is a small group of hired staff and student interns who work with clients and volunteers directly, including a client coordinator, a volunteer coordinator, a business manager, a weekend coordinator, and a chef. Also significant are the many local, national, and international individual volunteers and community partnerships that contribute to the shelter's mission to offer "a safe and welcoming home" that fosters "self-sufficiency and cultural integration" as well as values "which witness God's Providence in our world" (La Posada Providencia).

At the time that I began this project, most of the shelter clients were in some stage of their asylum process that they began prior to entering U.S. immigration detention facilities. During their stay at LPP, they typically awaited final decisions or approval to work in the United States. Common countries represented at the shelter are African: Democratic Republic of Congo, Eritrea, and Rwanda; Central American: Honduras, Guatemala, and Venezuela; and Eastern European: Russia and Ukraine. But at times, there are people from a variety of other nations as well, such as Haiti, Cuba, or China, adding to the dynamic experience of life at LPP. Still, because of the small size of the shelter and the well-established routine and schedule of each day, it serves as a stable refuge for the residents who experience the liminality inherent in displacement. At the time I completed this study (2017–2018), prior to "Remain in Mexico" (see Chapter 3), 67% of LPP clients stayed an average of three nights, others only stayed a day or two, while a few clients were considered long-term, staying for more than a month and even as long as over a year.

The shelter consists of four buildings that clients are allowed to access: Casa Belen (Figure 1.1) contains the main kitchen and dining area as well as staff offices for the client coordinator, business manager, and executive director.

Casa Carolina (Figure 1.2) is the building where single women with or without children reside in small, shared bedrooms, and this space also contains a living and kitchen area where women are able to help staff cook. Two of the Sisters who work at the shelter also have office spaces within Casa Carolina.

Casa Guillermo (Figure 1.3) is a building for single men or married men traveling with spouses, and it also contains small shared bedrooms.

The English language learning (ELL) classroom is housed in a portable building (Figure 1.4) where classes are held twice a day on weekdays.

While clients have space for individual or small group time, they often spend time together maintaining the shelter's steady rhythm through on-site gardening, household chores, and attending ELL classes. The outdoor spaces consist of multiple gardens of fruit, vegetables, and flowers (Figure 1.5), spaces for relaxation and socialization (Figure 1.6), as well as a few play areas with sports and playground equipment (Figure 1.7). Notably, the shelter sits on 10 acres of land on an isolated farm road. With no fencing, the property is green and expansive.

Figure 1.1 "*El Chef*/The Cook." A staff member cooking a meal in Casa Belen's kitchen. Photograph by Ayana.

Figure 1.2 "Casa Carolina." A small white house under a large tree in a green space. Photograph by Ayana.

Figure 1.3 "Casa Guillermo." A small house along a paved large driveway and a basketball hoop. Photograph by Ayana.

Figure 1.4 A circular table in the middle of the ELL classroom. Photograph by Michelle.

Figure 1.5 "Prayer" shows a donated statue of *La Virgen de Guadalupe* within the butterfly garden. Photo by Esther.

Figure 1.6 "*El Columpio*/The Swing" captures a large wooden portable porch swing outside of Casa Carolina. Photo by Ayana.

Figure 1.7 Casa Guillermo along the paved driveway and basketball hoop with green space in the background. Photograph by Amal.

Unexpected Agency within Liminal Contexts

There are many "shelters" in the world that offer respite for people seeking asylum, and the scholarship about life in these spaces often focuses on the challenges, such as individuals feeling restrained, inhibited, and powerless (Ghorashi et al.; Sampson et al.; Steimel, "Empowerment" and "Knowledges"). In their article, "Unexpected Agency on the Threshold: Asylum Seekers Narrating from an Asylum Seeker Centre," Ghorashi and colleagues elaborate on the atmosphere of uncertainty, disconnection, and limitation for opportunity (especially for work and mobility) which is often synonymous with shelter life. These conditions are associated with futility, desperation, and hopelessness, all hallmarks of the hegemonic displacement experience.

However, Ghorashi and colleagues also describe how liminal spaces of displacement, or the "in-between social structures" like shelters, may provide a time for reflection, choice making, and growth that highlight agency of people who are displaced (378). Their research indicates that residents of temporary facilities often exemplified an "inner world and powers of imagination," when hoping and planning about a life of resettlement and conventional agency (384).

I was inspired to learn more about how these "powers of imagination" build agency within these in-between spaces, so I leaned closely on Chicana Feminist works which grapple with liminality as a cornerstone of the Chicanx experience (Anzaldúa; Flores; Licona; Pérez; Zepeda). In her book, *The Decolonial Imaginary*, Emma Pérez argues how Third Space allows marginalized people room to "critique" and imagine "what has been, what is, and what many of us hope will be" because those who live in Third Space simultaneously "live the past, present, and future" (127). Third Space is a term that especially supports my analysis throughout this work; it is defined as a material or an imagined site in which individuals are allowed to "identify themselves as different from dominant culture and thus are able to establish self- and/or group autonomy because they name themselves" (Zepeda 142).

Additionally, previous scholarship has studied how the resistance that such spaces afford manifests through discourse; therefore, I looked to scholarship which demonstrates the variety of ways in which marginalized voices are able to center their own lived experiences in unconventional ways. As I completed this project, I aligned with feminist rhetorics perspectives on silence and listening from Cheryl Glenn and Kristina Ratcliffe, especially to help me formulate how silence works as an *echo of displacement*—or narratives and silences which reflect traces of or reverberated responses to the trauma of persecution and dislocations of home (Chapter 4). Such scholars argue that silence and listening "have been conceptualized and employed in different times and places by many different people—some with power, some without—for purposes as diverse as showing reverence, gathering knowledge, planning action, buying time, and attempting to survive" (Glenn and Ratcliffe 2).

Within this book, I also respond to feminist rhetoricians Sonja K. Foss and Cindy L. Griffin's call for an "invitational rhetoric" built on safety and understanding as an alternative to classical conceptions of rhetoric that primarily focus on persuasion through argumentation and control. Such ideas coincide with work done within displacement contexts from the social sciences which view silence as a strategy for displaced people within liminal communities to tell stories on their own terms and at their own pace (De Haene et al.; McFadyen; Puvimanasinghe et al.).

Scholars have additionally demonstrated how marginalized people compose a rhetoric of resistance through routines which afford feelings of agency. For example, refugee scholars Robyn C. Sampson and colleagues find that while in transit, people seeking asylum exhibit a "deep desire for progress in life's journey [which] led participants to undertake substantive life projects and to keep working towards a better future" (1136). In addition, rhetoric and communication scholar Sarah Steimel has skillfully argued how refugees within resettlement contexts push back against staff ideologies of Western "empowerment," resulting in clients manifesting their own "empowerment(s) in economic, educational, personal, and family terms" ("Empowerment" 90) often played out in the daily and routine aspects of life. Indeed, this book focuses on the day-to-day activities which allow new stories of resistance to manifest within a Third Space, especially because a shelter is a place where cooking, sleeping, praying, learning, arguing, laughing, and playing—life—happen. In fact, the day-to-day is given great significance in Chicana feminist scholarship because building "a home is a necessary step in the building of a Chicana feminist community in that the sense of belonging associated with home is often missing from their lives" including the familial relationships that may have been severed, such as the mother/child tie (Flores 149–50).

Therefore, this book engages with scholarship that values the power of routine in the formation of individual and collective identity (culture), mainly found in cultural rhetorics' scholarship like *The Practice of Everyday Life* by Michel de Certeau, as well as pieces by Andrea M. Riley-Mukavetz and the variety of works from Malea M. Powell and colleagues.

I appreciate how previous scholarship emphasizes the "doubleness of asylum seekers' agency" within transient spaces, especially because it draws attention to the fact that people seeking asylum are often "lacking agency to act regarding their position within legal or societal structures" and this positioning "enabled in them an agency rooted in finding themselves outside normalizing societal structures" (Ghorashi et al. 385). Indeed, the hegemonic narratives that often haunt people seeking asylum within legal and societal structures focus on fixedly categorizing them as ineffectual victims or frauds who are in need of the Global North for a life worth living (Rajaram; Steimel). As previous scholarship has affirmed, spending time in spaces like shelters provides people seeking asylum an opportunity to collaborate and push back against dominant discourses in order to (re)negotiate various forms of agency.

I build on this valuable work through collaborating with people seeking asylum and those who work with them in order to discuss their rhetorical roles in this liminal space of the asylum process. Specifically, this book contributes to people's own direct reflections on the rhetorical demands that a person seeking asylum in the U.S. faces. It also invites clients, staff, and volunteers to discuss how LPP, as a material site, assembles with many other networks and agents within the rhetorical ecology of the U.S. asylum system—from U.S. immigration policies and volunteers to everyday vibrant things such as the U.S. flag or cleaning supplies. This book argues how the underlying ideologies of tangible materiality liberate and constrain the stories the shelter composes about the asylum experience. In this way, I depend largely on utilizing ecology as a metaphor for understanding meaning-making (richly discussed in Chapter 2), especially informed by respective works from Jenny Edbauer, Nedra Reynolds, and Jane Bennett.

Chapter Layout

I have framed my book like many in the field of cultural rhetorics; I centralize the everyday stories of people. This is a strategic discursive move in that I am proposing an alternative rhetoric to displacement—a decolonial way to interact with the stories we hear about asylum by centering what has long been marginalized—the everyday humanity of those that are often only heard through their spectacular rhetorics of displacement.

In Chapter 2, "*La Mesa Redonda*: A Located-Listening Approach to Knowledge-Building," I discuss how my mixed-methodology and methods align with the project. I especially take time to describe how my approach to research was drawn from within the community itself, inspired by the material space. I delineate an exceptional and vibrant "thing" at the shelter that works as a metaphor for my methodology—*la mesa redonda*, or "the round table." I also use this chapter to position myself within the project as a contributor of knowledge.

Chapter 3, "*En la Frontera*: Resisting Spatial Conventions," examines how spaces and places of two distinct, yet overlapping rhetorical ecologies—the U.S. asylum system and the RGV where the shelter is located—work to perpetuate, resist, and complicate fixed labels for people seeking asylum. I use participant data to specifically describe how spaces like airports, border patrol holding cells, or detention centers perpetuate the ideology that people who seek asylum at national borders are criminals. In contrast, the RGV's positioning on the U.S.-Mexico border affords unique opportunities to revise such criminal labels, especially seen in how local advocacy groups use spaces like international bridges and border walls for alternative purposes, such as protest and education. In this way, the overlapping rhetorical ecologies of the RGV and the U.S. asylum process assemble together as a vibrant rhetorical exigence for LPP to manifest as a Third Space.

Chapter 4, "Public Narratives of Asylum & Silence as an Echo of Displacement," elucidates how, as part of a Third Space, the staff and volunteers within LPP provide opportunities for clients to construct their public narratives—narratives clients may use in their asylum applications—by first recognizing clients' *echoes of displacement*, or the stories which reflect traces of or reverberated responses to the trauma of persecution and dislocations of home. I argue that such an approach counters the ideology that the goal of storytelling is persuasion, and instead, storytelling at LPP is based on "invitational rhetoric" (Foss and Griffin) that makes space for the agency of clients' silences.

Chapter 5, "Cooking, Crocheting, *y Cantando*: Composing Agency through Routine," centers on the daily life of clients and attributes agency to their routines. By developing a "rhetoric of difference" (Flores) through shared routines like cooking, clients are able to foster identities which fracture hegemonic perspectives of people seeking asylum, especially the mainstream narrative centered on displaced people as victims who are only enabled through the nation-state. I explore three alternative narratives that manifest through routine: "I am useful," "I have a (temporary) family," and "I am patriotic without citizenship." I argue that these narratives are examples of *rasquache* storytelling practice at LPP in that they "make do" with the materials available for resistance (Medina-López).

Chapter 6, "The Long Path Out through Advocacy-Building," concludes the book by outlining my own departure from the research process, especially considering significant advocacy efforts developed from the project. The efforts I detail exemplify how building transnational rhetorical feminist literacies is a meaningful way to connect community advocacy work with the larger contexts, scales of power, and humanity of those whose lives are problematically marked by displacement.

This book demonstrates how people who seek asylum and those who work with them are the rhetorical and sociocultural experts on this issue; as such, the project highly values people's own direct analytical interpretations and creative contributions regarding the rhetorical and neocolonial narrative demands and liminal spaces that a person seeking asylum in the U.S faces.

Also, this study may add to the emerging importance of rhetoric within discussions of asylum and forced migration. Understanding the composing processes of people seeking asylum as a collection of complex cultural and rhetorical negotiations is significant because stories are often the most efficacious resource that a person seeking asylum has when applying for legal status, as they must use narrative to convince the U.S. government of their credible fear. Thus, this book suggests support for people seeking asylum to navigate the narrative struggles they face in the U.S.

Additionally, for rhetorical and/or forced migration scholars, this work demonstrates the significance of rhetorical ecology theory as part of a blended methodology in understanding people seeking asylum as a group in a perpetual and explicit state of ethos development. This perspective compels those who work with people seeking asylum—in governmental/institutional, advocacy/community-engaged learning, or research contexts—to revise and expand rhetorical data to include the wider networks in which these narratives are constructed. And for the specific, local community with which I collaborate, this work may not simply call attention to the varied narratives of displacement, but also affirm how their own cultural rhetorics allow clients and staff to create a necessary space of refuge, or a space that many simply call "home."

References

Anzaldúa, Gloria. *Borderlands/La Frontera: The New Mestiza*. Aunt Lute Books, 1987.

"Application for Asylum and for Withholding from Removal." *Department of Homeland Security U.S. Citizenship and Immigration Services, I-589*, https://www.uscis.gov/sites/default/files/files/form/i-589.pdf. Accessed 18 Jan. 2018.

Bennett, Jane. *Vibrant Matter: A Political Ecology of Things*. Duke University Press, 2010.

De Certeau, Michele. *The Practice of Everyday Life*. The University of California Press, 2011.

De Haene, Lucia, et al. "Holding Harm: Narrative Methods in Mental Health Research on Refugee Trauma." *Qualitative Health Research*, vol. 20, no. 12, 2010, pp. 1664–76.

Edbauer, Jenny. "Unframing Models of Public Distribution: From Rhetorical Situation to Rhetorical Ecologies." *Rhetoric Society Quarterly*, vol. 35, no. 4, 2005, pp. 5–24.

"Figures at a Glance." *UNHCR: UN Refugee Agency*, https://www.unhcr.org/us/about-unhcr/who-we-are/figures-glance.

Flores, Lisa A. "Creating Discursive Space through a Rhetoric of Difference: Chicana Feminists Craft a Homeland." *Quarterly Journal of Speech*, vol. 82, no. 2, 1996, pp. 142–56.

Foss, Sonja K., and Cindy L. Griffin. "Beyond Persuasion: A Proposal for an Invitational Rhetoric." *Communication Monographs*, vol. 62, 1995, pp. 2–18, *EBSCO*.

Ghorashi, Halleh, Marije de Boer, and Floor ten Holder. "Unexpected Agency on the Threshold: Asylum Seekers Narrating from an Asylum Seeker Centre." *Current Sociology*, vol. 66, no. 3, 2018, pp. 373–91. *Sage*, doi:10.1177/0011392117703766.

Glenn, Cheryl, and Krista Ratcliffe, editors. "Introduction: Why Silence and Listening are Important Rhetorical Arts." *Silence and Listening as Rhetorical Arts*, Southern Illinois University Press, 2011, pp. 1–19.

"La Posada Providencia." https://lppshelter.org/. Accessed 24 Apr. 2024.

Licona, Adela C. "(B)orderlands' Rhetorics and Representations: The Transformative Potential of Feminist Third-Space Scholarship and Zines." *NWSA Journal*, vol. 17, no. 2, 2005, pp. 104–29. *JSTOR*, https://www.jstor.org/stable/4317128.

McFadyen, Gillian. "Memory, Language and Silence: Barriers to Refuge within the British Asylum System." *Journal of Immigrant & Refugee Studies*, 2018, pp. 1–17. *Sage*, doi: 10.1080/15562948.2018.1429697.

Medina-López, Kelly. "Rasquache Rhetorics: A Cultural Rhetorics Sensibility." *Constellations*, vol. 1, no. 1, 2018, pp. 1–23. http://constell8cr.com/issue-1/rasquache-rhetorics-a-cultural-rhetorics-sensibility/.

Pérez, Emma. *The Decolonial Imaginary: Writing Chicanas into History (Theories of Representation and Difference)*. Indiana University Press, 1999.

Powell, Katrina M. *Identity and Power in Narratives of Displacement*. Routledge, 2015.

Puvimanasinghe, Teresa, et al. "Narrative and Silence: How Former Refugees Talk about Loss and Past Trauma." *Journal of Refugee Studies*, vol. 28, no. 1, 2015, pp. 69–92. *EBSCO*, doi: 10.1093/jrs/feu019.

Rajaram, Prem Kumar. "Humanitarianism and Representations of the Refugee." *Journal of Refugee Studies*, vol. 15, no. 3, 2002, pp. 247–64.

Reyes, Monica, et al. "Enacting Invitational Rhetorics: Leveraging Networks of Care in the U.S. Asylum Process." *Grassroots Activisms: Public Rhetorics in Localized Contexts*, edited by Lisa L. Phillips, et al., Ohio State UP, 2024, pp. 235–50.

Reynolds, Nedra. *Geographies of Writing: Inhabiting Places and Encountering Difference*. Southern Illinois UP, 2004.

Riley-Mukavetz, Andrea M. "Towards a Cultural Rhetorics Methodology: Making Research Matter with Multi-generational Women from the Little Traverse Bay Band." *Rhetoric, Professional Communication and Globalization*, vol. 5, no. 1, 2014, pp. 108–25.

Sampson, Robyn C., et al. "The Myth of Transit: The Making of a Life by Asylum Seekers and Refugees in Indonesia." *Journal of Ethnic & Immigration Studies*, vol. 42, no. 7, 2016, pp. 1135–52. *Sage*, doi: 10.1080/1369183X.2015.1130611.

Steimel, Sarah J. "Negotiating Refugee Empowerment(s) in Resettlement Organizations." *Journal of Immigrant & Refugee Studies*, vol. 15, no. 1, 2017, pp. 90–107. *Sage*, doi: 10.1080/15562948.2016.1180470.

Steimel, Sarah J. "Negotiating Knowledges and Expertise in Refugee Resettlement Organizations." *Cogent Social Sciences*, 2016, pp. 1–15. doi: https://doi.org/10.1080/23311886.2016.1162990.

The Cultural Rhetorics Theory Lab (Malea Powell, Daisy Levy, Andrea Riley-Mukavetz, Marilee Brooks-Gillies, Maria Novotny, Jennifer Fisch-Ferguson). "Our Story Begins Here: Constellating Cultural Rhetorics Practices." *Enculturation: A Journal of Rhetoric, Writing, and Culture*, vol. 18, no. 1, 2014, n.p. http://enculturation.net/our-story-begins-here.

U.S. Border Patrol Claims of Credible Fear Apprehensions by Sector." *U.S. Customs and Border Protection*. https://www.cbp.gov/newsroom/stats/southwest-land-border-encounters/usbp-sw-border-apprehensions.

Zepeda, Candace. "Chicana Feminism." *Decolonizing Rhetoric & Composition Studies*, edited by Iris D. Ruiz and Raul Sánchez, Palgrave Macmillan, 2019, pp. 137–51.

2 *La Mesa Redonda*

A Located-Listening Approach to Knowledge-Building

Like all cultural rhetorics (CR) scholars, I'm interested in stories. When I started learning about how people who seek political asylum in the U.S. are required to share their stories with government agencies about what led them to the U.S., I became fascinated by the contexts of their storytelling. I began to understand that people seeking asylum typically tell their stories during stressful governmental and legal interviews or within detailed persuasive writing on government applications. I obsessively read about how the stories required in these contexts reinforce reductive understandings about forced migration, and the stories seemed to be complex rhetorical acts that didn't exactly work "to heal, to teach, [or] to challenge dominant narratives" as stories often can (Hidalgo et al.). The truth is, the stories people seeking asylum tell within the U.S. asylum process must fit rigid, racist, neocolonial narrative standards about who is considered worthy of protection (Holland). What's more, these stories operate through the predominant classical ideology that persuasion and dominance are the goals of rhetoric.

While I discuss more about these rigid storytelling contexts in Chapter 4, this chapter explains how this CR project came together and the steps I took to complete it. In what follows, I first describe how I began volunteering at the shelter, including my problematic motivations for doing so. Then, I describe how significant a CR lens was for me to begin understanding why I had certain questions about the shelter, and how CR methodologies were best suited to help me pursue a collaborative research project with the community and make discoveries. Next, I describe how I designed my blended CR methodological approach, *located-listening*, by spending time with the LPP community at the shelter's round patio table, *la mesa redonda*, and valuing their stories. I explain how *located-listening*, as a CR research methodology, is designed to mirror the rhetorical practices at *la mesa redonda* which value material, equitable, accessible, and diverse contributions to knowledge. I discuss how the storytelling at *la mesa redonda* is a CR practice that critiques the hegemonic narratives about displacement.

DOI: 10.4324/9781003349693-2

Positioning Myself as a Contributor of Knowledge

Aligning with my assumptions that a researcher who works with people and their stories "does not collect narratives, but instead jointly participates in their construction and creation" (Loots et al. 110), it is necessary to examine how my role as a university-educated American woman working on a scholarly project may have impacted how the community perceived me as an interviewer and a listener of their migration experience. While I am not an immigrant, nor have I ever been displaced, my lived experiences as a woman of color living in a border community have prepared me to at least be intuitively sensitive to those who have been oppressed because of their language, gender, nationality, and race; I identify with feminist rhetorician Nedra Reynolds as she describes her position with people who participated in her own scholarship, "I was never 'one of them', but I shared their space and tried to pay attention" (*Geographies* 10). At the same time, I understand my position as an educated, U.S. citizen who teaches at a university, conducts research, and volunteers at the shelter communicates power, access, and privilege to the community.

I began volunteering as a way to connect with the world outside of my small community. As a young woman, I wasn't allowed to travel; my family operated through patriarchy, often referred to in our Mexican-American community as *machismo*, summed up by Anzaldúa in her discussion of "cultural tyranny" (38–40). My femaleness and my ethnicity, inextricably linked, were perceived as weaknesses, making me unfit to navigate the world without a male guide. So, I never left home to study, partly because in Mexican-American culture, when "a woman rebels, she is a *mujer mala*"[1] (Anzaldúa 39). While this choice I made may be perceived as weak, I can now appreciate that, like many people I have interviewed for this project, I was only operating under the cultural norms in which I existed at the time (Anzaldúa 42).

Later as a wife and stay-at-home mother caring for my two young daughters, I pursued a graduate degree in my hometown. The choice to stay behind positioned me to become the full-time primary caregiver to my mother-in-law as she battled cancer for two years and lived with my husband, daughters, and me. During this time, I learned much from her through the experience of caregiving; in fact, people would often say to me about my mother-in-law, "I am glad you were there for her." And *there* was home. At this point, I began to understand even more about how not only was my femaleness perceived as a major factor in how and where I am allowed to travel, but it is also a critical aspect of my perceived value as a woman who is able to stay behind to nurture and care for others. Similar to how Anzaldúa describes how the woman in Chicanx culture "exists first as kin … and last as self" (41), my "identity" was being continually established and negotiated through my "locatedness in various social and cultural 'spaces'" like home (Reynolds, "Location," 326) and places like my kitchen, my mother-in-law's oncologist's office, and the rocking chair where I put my daughters to sleep.

It was during this time that I also nurtured a longtime fascination with 19th century travel diaries, which I wrote about for my master's thesis. As I cared for my mother-in-law and children within my home, I found kinship with mothers I read about through many edited collections and primary sources in digital archives. I discovered that these women, like me, also traveled, stayed behind, read, and wrote according to the permission of their brothers, fathers, and husbands. Still, I longed to move; and because moving was increasingly out of reach, staying became more and more indicative of how I saw myself and how others saw me.

My volunteer work with LPP was also influenced by my home community of the RGV which has a clear history and sensibility to support people who migrate. This sensibility stems from the fact that our family members are transient. To put it plainly, for many people like me who call the RGV home, we aren't quite sure how to label our respective generations because our ancestors (*padres y abuelos*) moved, settled, and resettled across *la frontera* multiple times throughout their lives, so our migration stories are messy (Reyes and Nájera). However, over time I learned how the U.S. asylum system preferred neat and tidy (reductive) migration stories from those seeking asylum. I cared about how people seeking asylum were required to tell such stories, and if they had the rhetorical tools to do so.

I first heard about *La Posada Providencia* (LPP) through a *National Public Radio* broadcast while driving to my job as a lecturer at a community college one morning (Inskeep). This 2013 "Morning Edition" episode featured Saraa who had traveled from Ethiopia to Sudan to Brazil and then through Venezuela, Colombia, and eventually up through Mexico to the U.S. southern border. When I heard about her journey, and how the shelter staff had offered her refuge in our rural area of south Texas, I was shocked. I had no idea that my border community was a crossing point for a variety of people from many countries, not just the U.S. and Mexico. I called the shelter, visited the following week, and began volunteering inconsistently. Then in 2017, my teaching load became more manageable and my daughters were older, so my volunteer work became steady. Over the next two years, I visited the shelter two hours at a time, at least once a week, helping with small office tasks, caring for children, tutoring adults, and connecting staff to community resources.

I would usually spend my time in the English Language Learning (ELL) class; and even though I don't speak Spanish well and most clients arrived from Spanish-speaking countries, the clients and I found ways to communicate grounded in patience and empathy. In fact, speaking Spanish with many of the clients at the shelter was a material opportunity for me to offset insider/outsider power dynamics. Almost every time I sat with a client for language tutoring and admitted to them that my Spanish was a work in progress, they would look relieved. In that moment of my vulnerability, clients understood that, like them, I was also learning how to communicate. With a smile, nearly every resident offered a reciprocal teaching experience: "*Si tu me enseñas Inglés, yo te ayudo con tu Espanol*."[2]

Despite my connection with clients through language learning, I still exhibited privilege through U.S. citizenship and socioeconomic stability. Personally, my "privilege" is most clear in my initial motivation to volunteer at LPP. I wanted to interact with people from outside my small community, extending from my desire to travel, but that motivation became problematic for me. For one, I started to wonder how being a volunteer with certain entitlements that come from U.S. citizenship and education, albeit a woman of color, among people in such precarious circumstances, often from the Global South, plays into humanitarian dynamics which perpetuate inequality. I found that I was continually attempting to be accountable for how my identity, positioning, and location (across various points) inform and motivate my relationship and scholarship with the shelter. In "Notes Toward a Politics of Location," feminist poet Adriene Rich advocates for writers and scholars to be accountable for their overlapping identities as a "struggle to keep moving, a struggle to accountability" (211). In fact, I still struggle and grapple with my motivations for volunteerism and scholar-activism, which is a humbling process.

What I do know is that with time, frequent visits, and conversations, the staff and the clients became more than reductive and sensationalized stories. Over time, I learned more about clients apart from their traumatic journeys and experiences. I shared time with them in their daily lives as they/we cared for their kids, ate, studied, offered advice, sang, played, and prayed. In other words, the daily practices I shared with clients and staff helped me appreciate more deeply their humanity. I wanted others to understand that the clients were not simply "asylum seekers." They are complex individuals with diverse stories, individual dreams, skills, backgrounds, and personalities. Such an observation aligns with CR scholars such as Malea Powell and Andrea Riley-Mukavetz who advocate for "relationality and there-ness" (Riley-Mukavetz 108) through listening to the everyday practices and stories of a community.

Meanwhile, clients and staff had approached me about how my work as an "English teacher" could help them. Clients would often ask for my writing help when they were trying to compose their stories for lawyers, and staff would point me out in the ELL classroom as a "professional." It seemed like LPP was eager to connect my professional work to their everyday needs.

While I was developing a familiar and caring relationship with the people there, I had no plans to collaborate with the shelter for research. Although I wanted to focus on displacement narratives for my dissertation, I was uneasy about collaborating with the shelter because of the risks of "romanticizing mobility and hybrid identities, and tokenizing individual writers over and above a contextual and geopolitical analysis of alternative rhetorical practices" (Hesford and Schell 462). In her essay, "Cosmopolitanism and the Geopolitics of Feminist Rhetoric," Hesford also warns about "Western-centric cosmopolitan narratives that romanticize certain forms of travel and engagement with non-Western subjects" (53). Hesford and Schell borrow from composition scholar Deepika Bahri to remind scholar-activists to be "mindful of uncritical cosmopolitanisms and the 'baggage of voyeurism and self-exculpation' [Bahri 80] which configures scholars, teachers, and students as cultural travelers and the cultures and peoples of the postcolony as static entities" (Hesford and Schell 463). At the same time, I understood that LPP is a unique community which would offer crucial insights into the asylum experience if I could be patient enough to deeply listen to those at LPP as experts on the issue.

I approached LPP staff, and I asked them about their needs and how someone like me, who is interested in writing and how stories are told, can help answer questions they have about the shelter. The director shared her earnest questions about what the staff were doing well at the shelter and what more could be done to help support clients who were working on their stories. Over months, I worked with the feedback from LPP and created research questions aligned with the community's expressed needs and questions.

With faculty and shelter support, I completed a pilot study in the Spring of 2018. I was able to complete four private, semi-structured interviews with LPP clients which focused on how each person interpreted the credible fear interview and the U.S. asylum process as well as how the shelter space supported their journeys. This focus allowed the community to reflect on the rhetorical challenges and affordances of telling their stories in such high-stakes contexts. I also asked each participant what they thought was most important for people to know about their lives, their stories, and their experience with pursuing asylum in the U.S. The pilot was an attempt to better align this project with what the people experiencing the U.S. asylum process—the first-hand experts—considered relevant to critique, contextualize, and clarify the storytelling that happens in order to access protection. The questions I was asking demonstrated a CR approach in that they centered stories of the community in order to "delink from the mechanisms of colonialism" (Bratta and Powell).

Indeed, my time at the shelter helped me understand CR as a practice. I learned through joining this community that as we live and work collectively within specific communities, we build culture and make meaning (*do* rhetoric) through relationships, symbols, material conditions, locations, and ordinary day-to-day practices. In other words, culture is rhetorical and rhetoric is cultural. I paid attention to how individual and community rhetorical practices create culture and how that culture affects meaning-making and identity. I examined how the variety of spaces and places individuals and communities inhabit—from kitchens to classrooms—influence cultural-rhetorical practices. A key goal of CR is the analysis of systemic power and its effects on cultural-rhetorical practices in specific communities. This would require me to learn more about CR as a methodology.

Cultural Rhetorics Methodologies

CR scholars like me maintain that research should be done in communities in which we are already a part. Researching with communities in which we already have established and accountable relationships means we have experience observing, listening to, participating with, and learning from the cultural community. Having a relationship with the cultural community helps scholars to think about the individuals who will "be impacted by what [we are] researching and writing" as well as the ethical ways in which we ask our questions and disseminate knowledge (Arellano et al.). Having a relationship means we are curious about and personally engage in the meaning-making practices of the cultural communities we study (Riley-Mukavetz 110).

I affirm this principle, and like Riley-Mukavetz, I am curious how CR scholars can not only study such meaning-making practices but also "mirror" these same practices in our research approaches. Such mirroring will allow us to relinquish control of the research approach "to the people we write with and about" (Arellano et al.).

Mirroring is also an act of accurately esteeming the cultural community as experts in their own lives. It is a rhetoric of respect. Indeed, Riley-Mukavetz writes about the realization that her research respondents "had more experience with community-based research than [she] did"; she esteemed the community she studied as "intellects who understood disciplinary conversations on ethical research methodologies and representations of American Indians in formal education" (115).

Relinquishing control also means being flexible and adapting, or "making space for a myriad of kinds of knowledge making, research methodologies, community understandings, etc." (Hidalgo et al.). When researchers willingly hold on to preset expectations about the cultural community and *how* the community will respond to research questions, we are continuing a colonial approach to knowledge-making. When we disregard the responses from the community that don't seem to (initially) make sense or *fit* the narratives we've heard, we perpetuate reductive knowledge. Reductive knowledge is clean, tidy, and easy to write about. Listening to and writing about the varied embodied stories of the cultural communities we work with takes time, revision, and reflexivity.

Storytelling is a significant rhetoric for LPP and one that I aimed to mirror in my research approach. Storytelling happens in the kitchen and in the dorms. Stories flow on the playgrounds and in the ELL classrooms. I heard stories about life before displacement as well as the horrors, tragedy, and hope of displacement. I heard stories about hobbies, education, goals, children, sickness, pregnancy, rape, and death. Most of the storytelling I observed happened around *la mesa redonda*, a circular outdoor table located under a large oak tree (Figure 2.1).

La Mesa Redonda/The Round Table

The round patio table is one of the first things I see when I would drive onto the shelter's property (Figure 2.1). The simple and sturdy thing was a common meeting place for clients to catch up throughout the day. There are many times I used this table to talk with clients as well, especially when the weather was nice, or if the ELL classroom was too crowded. Indeed, I had many vulnerable talks at this table with the people of LPP long before the research began.

The clients have also shared how important this table is in forming a sense of community at LPP (Chapter 4), so I considered how it may work as a metaphor for this project because of the ways it so fittingly represents how I blend various theoretical lenses in my approach to knowledge-building. What initially caught my attention was how the circular design connotes equality: each person is able to have a full view of the others seated, so the conversation can be easily shared; however, it is also a permeable space because the bench design provides access for people to come and go. The very architecture of the piece makes it a shared and accessible space for the diverse people who stay at the shelter. I wanted the architecture of the research approach to have similar characteristics, so I created a blended CR research approach, relying on two theoretical lenses—rhetorical ecology and Chicana feminism.

Figure 2.1 "*La Mesa Redonda*"/"The Round Table" shows a white circular outdoor table with connected curved benches on the patio outside Casa Carolina. Photo by Esther.

I blend rhetorical ecology's argument that meaning is made through shifting, intertwined, located contexts that are formed through a variety of humans, non-humans, and sociopolitical conditions (Bennett; Edbauer) with Chicana feminism's emphasis on the rhetorical possibility and agency of (dis)located and marginalized people within liminal spaces. Thus, I have designed *located-listening* as a CR research approach that understands knowledge-building as grounded in four axioms: materiality, equitability, permeability, and diversity. Each of these axioms makes way for the formation of rhetorical networks which have the power to influence the wider rhetorical ecology in which they exist, the U.S. asylum system.

Materiality: Understanding Knowledge-Building as Located and Embodied

The table, situated in the shade of a large oak tree between Casa Belen (community building) and Casa Carolina (the women's dorm), affords certain rhetorical possibilities because of its location, shape, and size. I have often wondered how the table's design and location are essential in understanding what meaning is able to be made there. As Nedra Reynolds argues, "the [material] spaces of the everyday," like *la mesa redonda*, "demand equal, urgent attention" to the spaces of imagination (*Geographies* 14).

Materiality argues that the physical, environmental, biological, sexual, economic, sociopolitical, and historical conditions affect how meaning is made. What this means is that rhetoric is bound up in material positioning, beginning with physical bodies and extending to geographical location and the material conditions which surround it. For posthumanist and new materialist scholars, like Bennett, Haraway, and Gruwell, all objects, not just those like *la mesa redonda*, contain the ability to be effectively rhetorical and have the potential to be part of the rhetorical moment because they carry meaning in and of themselves.

Bennett argues that objects contain an "energetic vitality" or "thing power" which is often realized through their assemblages with other objects and creatures (5). In this way, rhetorical exchange or meaning-making is not simply dependent on human involvement; instead, there is agency within the relationships between all matter—humans, non-humans, objects, and spaces.

By blending Chicana feminist perspectives with a rhetorical ecology approach, I understood materiality in terms of embodiment or what Chicana feminist Cherrie Moraga simply calls a "theory in the flesh" which is a theory "where the physical realities of our lives—our skin color, the land or concrete we grew up on, our sexual longings—all fuse to create a politic out of necessity" (23). Chicana feminism's perspective of embodiment, which often uses displacement, migration, and borders as material contexts for their individual and collective rhetorical possibilities, adds to rhetorical ecology's perspective of materiality in ways necessary to this project.

This blend helps me see the community's expertise as grounded in their embodied experiences within the various geographies and material spaces they have traversed, including the shelter space itself (Cruz 658–9). In other words, I understand that the stories and silences that the community contributes have been first realized by and within their own bodies, especially bodies which have faced displacement from homes and families (Anzaldúa, *Caras* xxii). I recognize that each individual community member's body—especially as a *migrating body*—has acted and been "acted upon by the political and economic forces of globalization" making each body an "agent, witness, and provocateur" (Cruz 660) and a contributor to knowledge.

Equitable, Permeable, and Diverse: Understanding That Knowledge-Building Is Networked

In addition to embracing that knowledge stems from material and embodied lived experiences, a *located-listening* approach to knowledge-building also values diverse contributions that are forged through equitable and permeable distributed rhetorical networks. *La mesa redonda* lends itself to an equitable perspective of everyone gathered around it, exemplifying everyone's shared contributions toward making meaning in the space. In the same way, my blended approach to knowledge-building refuses a reductive cause-and-effect perspective; instead, located-listening sees that knowledge-building is shared and distributed through networks, or the fluctuating connections made between a variety of human and non-human things in a rhetorical context. If people and things are valued as equitable contributors of knowledge, it becomes more and more difficult to allot credit for knowledge to any one rhetor. Rather than considering simple cause-and-effect relationships, object-oriented ontologists, posthumanists, and new materialists problematize the role of intentionality and agency because, as Bennet puts it, "origin is a complex, mobile, and heteronomous enjoiner of forces" (33). Bennett argues that "there was never a time when human agency was anything other than an interfolding network of humanity and nonhumanity" (31). Rhetorical agency is distributed in that it is not "the product of independent human agents [;] rhetoric is instead a continual process that emerges from the intra-actions of human and nonhuman agents (who themselves are in a continual process of becoming through their intra-actions)" (Gruwell 15). In this way, *located-listening* understands that there is no solitary agent or even a hierarchical relationship between rhetors (22), but that all are composed of various pieces, like a "mosaic" (21). Thus, *located-listening* requires a patient tracing of contextual rhetorical assemblages of the stories the community shared.

Permeability refers to how the table's curved and split bench design allows each individual to enter and exit the conversations with ease; thus, the breaks in the seating are seen as organic paths in and out, quite fitting for the transience of the LPP community. I am inspired by this regard to permeability in knowledge-building because I understand rhetorical networks are perpetually in flux, as connections between rhetorical agents move. Located-listening adopts rhetorical ecology's argument that transience is an organic means of network formation. In other words, the assemblages or "bodies of relationships" that rhetors form with their material surroundings "shift as new bodies are introduced or subtracted" (Rice 208). Permeability also means leaving room for the "unpredictable" fluctuations in rhetorical assemblages, common in the precarious lives of displaced individuals (Gruwell 20).

Diversity refers to the varied people and stories that circulate at this table every day; as the shelter hosts a myriad of people from many geographical regions, those who sit at the table speak about diverse experiences, often in many languages. But diversity in this project is more than just linguistic or geographic variety; I see diversity more about how the stories at the table may push back against preconceived labels, blurring or fracturing the agent and victim binary surrounding the asylum experience. I see diversity as necessary for knowledge-building because heterogeneous actors and stories allow messy and contradictory multivocality which affords a decolonial conversation to erupt.

Of course, for Chicana feminists, diversity of experience is often painfully interwoven with personal transience and permeability within and across rhetorical networks, especially networked geographical and cultural borders. Anzaldúa, who famously compares the Rio Grande River in south Texas to a flesh wound, details how this boundary separates "a culture" that extends throughout her body: "staking fence rods in my flesh/splits me splits me" (24). However, Anzaldúa reaffirms there is value in the knowledge that is formed out of such transience because it is often multifaceted, messy, and non-binary, or what I see as decolonial for survival:

> She learns to be an Indian in Mexican culture; to be Mexican from an Anglo point of view. She learns to juggle cultures. She has a plural personality. She operates in a pluralistic mode—nothing is thrust out, the good the bad and the ugly, nothing rejected, nothing abandoned. Not only does she survive contradictions, she turns the ambivalence into something else.
> (Anzaldúa 79)

Indeed, Cindy Cruz has observed how Moraga's reliance on a theory of the flesh demonstrates how the body is a repository of multivocality: "[e]ach component of the brown body has its own story to tell—the lesbian mouth, the bent back in the fields, the dismembered daughter—and its deconstruction is a necessary process of reclaiming and re-imagining the histories and forms of agencies of women who are unrepresented and unheard" (Cruz 663).

Located-listening begins with valuing how meaning-making is bound up in material positioning, beginning with physical bodies and extending out to sociopolitical climates, geographical locations, as well as race, gender, sexuality, age, and (dis)ability. The bodies of those who participated in the study are contributors of knowledge in that they have been the material locus of power and subjugation associated with forced displacement; thus, their bodies are crucial contributors of knowledge. In addition, located-listening refuses a reductive cause-and-effect perspective of my participant's experiences and perspectives and instead values how meaning-making is distributed through networks or the fluctuating connections made between a variety of human and non-human things in a rhetorical context. Moreover, located-listening helps me understand that as displaced people move in the world, their rhetorical networks also move and transform, affecting how they are able to make meaning within new contexts. This movement, while jolting and often painful, affords dynamic and multifaceted rhetorics in that it highlights how clients who participated do not operate with fixed identities and narratives; they contain a plurality that has helped them survive their displacement.

Third Space

When studying the rhetorics of LPP, it was important to observe how the physical site creates paths for imagined possibilities and rhetorical practices (Licona 105). I understand that as people locate themselves within their physical surroundings and assemble materially with other bodies and things, there are opportunities for resistance and agency, revealing ideologies that are fostered or challenged within the community through what Chicana feminists refer to as "a differential consciousness" or a "Third Space consciousness," "capable of engaging creative and coalitional forms of opposition to the limits of dichotomous (mis)representations" (Licona 105). This differential consciousness manifests when individuals living outside the center, such as those in the LPP community, slip between cultural, linguistic, and rhetorical representations of authenticity or legitimacy of either side of a border and instead begin to rely on their own transcendent "perspectives, lived experiences, and rhetorical performances" which are birthed within the liminal spaces of borders (Licona 105).

For Chicana feminists, Third Space describes "the consciousness of marginalized individuals residing in proximity to real-and-imagined (b) orderland Geographies" (Zepeda 145); however, it also specifically makes room for discussions about "the lived experiences of difference such as race, culture, nation, class, sexual orientation and gender" (Zepeda 138). While Flores does not use the term Third Space, she understands that a "rhetoric of difference" leads to or is enabled by a rhetor establishing their own space which operates outside of binary oppositions; and through community, this space ultimately functions as a "home" (149) which is able to build bridges of alliances of kinship to other marginalized communities, cultures, and subjects (151).

Methods

After formulating the project's methodological approach, I turned my attention to how I would collect evidence (methods). Because I conducted feminist archival work prior to this project, I had learned how working with people's stories carries an overwhelming responsibility to "shape-re-member-[an alternative] rhetorical presence" (Glenn 8), especially in the work of marginalized voices, such as people seeking asylum. Conducting research with first-person narratives inspired me to ask valuable questions of myself such as: "Who is doing the representing, who is being represented, and how those structured positions are aligned with wider structures of power?" (Lisle 69).

Additionally, designing methods with displaced populations presented unique ethical challenges. I had to consider how displaced people often have liminal or no political rights; additionally, the research sites themselves may not be able to offer any support to the participants in that they may be experiencing sociopolitical conflict; research organizations may not have clear guidelines for their networked scholars about working with displaced people (Leaning 1432).

There are a handful of basic ethical considerations that scholars confront when researching displacement, revolving around four issues: (1) privacy and trust; (2) equitable, informed recruitment and willing participation; (3) potential harms and benefits; and (4) the place of advocacy within scholarship. Confidentiality involves researchers building and maintaining trust and privacy about a participant's identity or parts of their story which may cause them harm if exposed (Bloom 59–60; Clark-Kazak 13; Refugee Studies Centre 164, 166; Smith 67–68). Aside from using pseudonyms and communicating efforts to store data securely (which is important), Valerie J. Smith focuses on how researchers should provide assurances of confidentiality, explaining the reasons for questions, treating the interviewee as a valuable teacher, and occasionally feeling free to disclose reciprocal demographic information that shows commonality between the interviewer and the interviewee—if asked to do so and when appropriate (67–68).

Another issue is maintaining an atmosphere of voluntary consent and autonomous participation (Bloom 60; Clark-Kazak 12–13; Leaning 1433; Refugee Studies 165; Smith 64, 66), as there is a real danger of misinformed or coerced recruitment and participation when working with displaced people. Christina Clark-Kazak recommends that clear, ongoing communication with participants and any gatekeeping institutions and organizations is the best approach to ensuring participants understand their rights in participating, withdrawing, and receiving compensation (12). Additionally, Bloom contends that when researchers prohibit certain people from participating in research studies, they are only continuing to silence vulnerable populations through their own Western, patriarchal authority (59). Even when this is done in an effort to protect certain members of the research community, it only "feed[s] back into an assumption of such individuals not as subjects, but as objects, of research" (59).

Reducing psychological distress due to recalling and retelling painful stories or events (Clark-Kazak 13; Leaning 1433) is another consideration, as an interview question may bring up difficult experiences of loss, violence, and fear. Leaning anticipates this reaction and prompts researchers to consider what supports are in place for participants, as in counseling services (1433).

Understanding the relationship between research and advocacy (Bloom 59; Clark-Kazak 11; Refugee Studies 170–1) is yet another complex matter. Bloom's argument is clear that work with displaced populations should result in advocacy work and revision of policies, and Clark-Kazak urges data to be shared in a "timely manner" in order for participants and partners to consider the research findings (11).

While these considerations were daunting, I found that the shelter staff seemed to naturally understand many of these best practices, and I realize that it is their years of daily experience with displaced people that informed their perspectives; they patiently offered ideas about conducting private interviews, recruitment, and time constraints. After staff reviewed the study design, they shared a private office for me to use while conducting interviews, and they advised me about how to respond to clients who may become distressed while recounting their stories. Additionally, they helped me connect with clients after their arrival who fit recruitment criteria and allowed me to advertise the study within on-site language classes. They especially helped me connect with clients who were planning to stay at the shelter for a period of time that would allow them to participate. Their support was unwavering.

Operationalizing Located-Listening: Data Collection

Because this project focuses on how LPP functions as a site of rhetorical negotiation within the U.S. asylum system, I conducted two different types of interviews: one with staff, interns, or volunteers and another with residents who are currently in the asylum process (see Appendix B). With LPP clients, I conducted a preliminary interview followed by a visualization activity of their choice: completing a drawing or taking photos of the shelter. In the preliminary interview, I asked folks about their journey to the U.S. and LPP, and afterward, as they told their story, I asked more in-depth questions about the shelter space to help them generate ideas for their visualization. Next, I asked them to sketch or photograph LPP, especially including what they consider important spaces at the shelter. I emphasized that the visualization could take any shape or form most comfortable and meaningful to them, but that it should showcase those areas at the shelter where they experience freedom to talk, receive or ask for help in their asylum process, and plan for their future.

Only one person chose the drawing option for which I provided paper as well as colorful pencils and markers. For the photography option, I provided a digital camera for 48 hours, allowing time for them to also write or consider a brief comment or caption for each photo describing why they took it and what they wish the photograph to say in relation to their lives at the shelter.

These methods correspond with located-listening in a few ways, namely, that they give room for material, equitable, diverse, and permeable perspectives about a complex problem.

First, the visualization exercise provided LPP clients an opportunity to non-verbally articulate about the spaces and everyday material networks which they find meaningful (Bagnoli; Brennan-Horley and Gibson; McLees). These methods center on individuals capturing their material positioning and how their embodied perspectives of the space help them make meaning.

Next, by utilizing an art-based approach to knowledge-making, the project allowed for more equity by including diverse approaches to contribute to an issue that is predominately understood through quantifiable measures from governmental agencies. Also, in order to trace their "layers of experience" (Bagnoli 548) and perspectives of LPP as a rhetorical network, these visualizations allowed folks to "make sense of personal experiences which are also societally defined … and taken-for-granted [such as those of an asylum seeker]. This approach can reveal points of disjunction and overlap between societally dominant, powerful discourses, normative assumptions and individual, everyday experiences" (Miller 40). This art-based approach has some similarities to Arellano's "quilting as method" or QAM in her work with communities seeking to listen to stories of those who passed while migrating into the U.S. Arellano elaborates on how the quilts were efforts to use "incomplete data to construct non-linear narratives that allow for interpretation and provide a deeper understanding of why quantitative data about migrant deaths are incomplete and insufficient alone" (19). Certainly, art-based approaches have the potential for individuals to exercise a measure of autonomy in the contributions of their perspectives.

Moreover, the approach left room for the permeability of the rhetorical ecology. By allowing 48 hours, I left enough room for the unpredictability that is often part of life for displaced people and the rhetorical assemblages that they must inhabit. Gruwell argues that the unpredictability of the assemblage is valuable in that it fosters novel ways of perceiving the world and creating knowledge (20).

Once someone was done taking photos or drawing, I asked them to describe what they created in their own words. Because the interview was designed as semi-structured, the flow of the conversation was often shared between us naturally. After the participant described the visual(s), I then asked them specifically about their time at LPP, especially about the challenges and opportunities of composing their narratives and applications within the shelter as a liminal space.

Unlike clients, shelter staff were not asked to create a visualization of the shelter site due to time constraints in their schedules; the questions focused on their role and support in the formation of residents' asylum narratives as well as their perceptions of what constitutes an example of a successful asylum experience.

Everyone who participated in this study were adults and received approved notification about the project, including methods of data collection, audiotaping, as well as information about free counseling services if they were to experience negative emotions in connection to sharing their stories. In the end, a total of 17 people participated: 11 clients (five men and six women) representing nine countries from six different geographical regions; three full-time staff members (of which one was also a previous client); two seasonal volunteers; and one student intern.

Analysis

I decided that critical discourse analysis would best help me analyze both participant interviews and their visualizations because it scrutinizes how ideology and context are connected to language. In addition, because clients discuss their own photos in a post-interview, I am able to take both their visualizations and spoken interpretations through this type of analysis because "[d]iscourses are articulated through all sort of visual and verbal images and texts, specialized or not, and also through the practices that those languages permit" (Rose 136).

In *Visual Methodologies: An Introduction to Researching with Visual Materials*, Gillian Rose defines discourse as "groups of statements which structure the way a thing is thought, and the way we act on the basis of that thinking" (136). Rose's definition of discourse analysis aligns with critical discourse analysis (Cameron) because Rose strongly emphasizes how power is exercised through discourse. In language, power works at the ideological level, which is a key focus of critical discourse analysis: "CDA's concern [is] with the 'hidden agenda' of discourse, its ideological dimension" (Cameron 123). Angela M. Haas explains how "it is the rhetorical work that marks those cultural values—that makes explicit the ways in which subjectivities, positionalities, and commitments to particular knowledge systems are interrelated and situated within networks of power and geopolitical landbases—that I consider to be cultural rhetorics scholarship" (Cobos et al. 145).

Additionally, critical discourse analysis pays attention to context (Cameron 138), similar to Rose's argument that visual interpretation should pay attention to the "social location" in order to understand how a "discourse's production is important … in its effects" (159). One of the benefits of a critical discourse analysis approach is that it "pays careful attention to images themselves, and to the web of intertextuality in which any individual image is embedded" (Rose 161); however, Rose suggests that drawbacks of CDA's contextual approach are its "refusal to ascribe causality" and knowing "where to stop making intertextual connections" (162). These "drawbacks" are, in my opinion, points of strength in this analytical approach. Refusing to "ascribe causality" aligns most smoothly with rhetorical ecology methodology, new materialist rhetorics, and CR because it is not interested in cause-and-effect relationships which may lead to simplistic explanations of individuals' lived experiences; instead, this method focuses on the myriad of assemblages, located through patiently surveying contexts which constellate to make meaning.

In the preliminary and post-interviews with clients, I asked questions that helped them describe their analytical perspectives. For example, I commonly asked folks during the post-interview about why the photos they took were significant enough to share or what they liked about the photo or drawing.

The second half of the analysis involved looking for patterns, both in the photo content and the clients' preliminary and post-interviews. I used the deductive approach to discourse analysis Rose suggests when working with visuals as it is consistent with my approach of located-listening. Specifically, critical discourse analysis allowed me to locate "a regular pattern in a particular text or set of texts (involving lexis, grammar, modes of address, intertextual relations with other texts and genres, etc.)," leading to "an interpretation of the pattern, an account of its meaning and ideological significance" (Cameron 137). However, because the clients that I worked with were transient and in flux, the coding portion of the analysis was not a shared experience, and many of my clients had already moved on from the shelter when I began open coding. As the breaks in the benches of the outdoor circular table allow, this study is sensitive to the fact that these individuals were in a transient process.

I was inspired by sociologist David Karp's practical explanation of the coding process, as described in Hesse-Biber's *Feminist Research Practice*. I began the coding process by listening to the audio-recorded interviews three distinct times. During the first listening, I did not transcribe or take notes. Rose urges researchers at this stage to "forget all preconceptions you might have about the materials you are working with [by] allow[ing] this process of reading and looking to take its time … look and look again at the images" (150). While I agree that this process should take its time, I argue that there is value in listening to my own preconceptions, and I aimed to let those preconceptions rise to the surface as I listened to folks' stories during the first playback of each recording. I actively acknowledged my biases, assumptions, and tensions through journaling, as facing my preconceptions allowed me to interrogate and trace them in order to overcome them more meaningfully. During the second listening, I wrote down "idea memos" (Karp in Hesse-Biber 223) also referred to as "analytical memos" (Johnson 127) to focus on emerging patterns of ideas from the community. Rose explains that researchers at this point should "identify key themes, which may be key words, or recurring visual images. Make a list of these words or images and then go through all your sources, coding the material every time that word or image occurs. Then start to think about connections between and among key words and key images" (150). At this point, I considered the major directions, surprises, and emerging ideas of each interview.

The final listening was for interview transcriptions and further memo writing, based on theme (Karp in Hesse-Biber 223). At this point, I "listen[ed] to the fresh codes that emerge from the subsequent coding, and allow[ed] the new questions, details and paths to lead" my interpretation (Rose 154) in order to locate themes. Cameron explains that CDA involves a two-step process in which researchers identify "a regular pattern in a particular text or set of texts (involving lexis, grammar, modes of address, intertextual relations with other texts and genres, etc.)," followed by "proposing an interpretation of the pattern, an account of its meaning and ideological significance" (137). Once I established themes in the discourse, I began "to theorize about how a particular discourse works to persuade" (Rose 154). Some helpful questions I used to help me listen at this point were:

- "How does [this discourse] produce its effects of truth?" (157)
- What is not seen or said? What is not shown in these images? (158)
- How does this story or visual "provide a counterstory to the hegemonic narrative in circulation"? (156)
- What seems complex or contradictory about this story or visual? (156)

I compared themes across all participant interviews, allowing me to identify the shared ideologies associated with the everyday collaborative practices at the shelter.

To help me in this multistep process, I recorded my coding notes on a blog. The blog site's tagging feature helped me archive entries by participant tags (pseudonyms used) as well as theme tags for easy reference throughout coding. Although the people who participated were not involved in the coding, I used their own words to establish codes, otherwise known as "in vivo coding" (Johnson 123–4). The blog's tagging featured a word cloud format, which helped me keep track of the codes that were more common and those that tagged unique or one-of-a-kind insights. I then selected vivid, compelling sections of participants' stories to represent the most common codes, and this allowed me to formulate a working definition of the codes which were altered slightly throughout the writing. As definitions were in flux, the stories I leaned on to exemplify concepts also changed. As noted in Chapter 1, this project includes ample stories from the community in order to center their versions and expertise of their own lived experiences.

Conclusion

This chapter has thoroughly described how my alignment with CR has informed my reliance on methodologies which privilege how knowledge-building is material, shared, and networked. Observing such embodied systems helps researchers understand the possibilities for rhetorical agency. Because located-listening allows me to seek and rethink origins or "causal relations" (Biesecker 114) of meaning-making in the context of the U.S. asylum process, I view this approach as an answer to Gayatri Spivak's critical concern of how the relationship between postcolonial critic and the subaltern is similar to a mere echo with only traces of meaning. Additionally, I understand that my methodological approach is unique to this project, at this time and in this space.

In the following chapter, I take up the concepts of space and place even more specifically to show how the Rio Grande Valley, the area where the shelter is located, works to foster diverse stories and plural identities that resist reductive approaches to understanding the nuance of asylum experience.

Notes

1 "bad woman."
2 "If you teach me English, I will help you with your Spanish."

References

Anzaldúa, Gloria. *Borderlands/La Frontera: The New Mestiza*. Aunt Lute Books, 1987.

Anzaldúa, Gloria. Introduction. *Making Face, Making Soul: Haciendo Caras*. Aunt Lute Foundation Books, 1990, pp. xv–xxviii.

Arellano, Sonia, et al. "Ethically Working within Communities: Cultural Rhetorics Methodologies Principles." *Constellations*, vol. 4, 2021, https://constell8cr.com/conversations/cultural-rhetorics-methodologies/

Bagnoli, Anna. "Beyond the Standard Interview: The Use of Graphic Elicitation and Arts-based Methods." *Qualitative Research*, vol. 9, no. 5, 2009, pp. 547–70. *Sage*, doi: 10.1177/1468794109343625.

Bennett, Jane. *Vibrant Matter: A Political Ecology of Things*. Duke University Press, 2010.

Biesecker, Barbara. "Rethinking the Rhetorical Situation from within the Thematic of 'Différance.'" *Philosophy & Rhetoric*, vol. 22, no. 2, 1989, pp. 110–30.

Bloom, Tendayi. "Asylum Seekers: Subjects or Objects of Research?" *American Journal of Bioethics*, vol. 10, no. 2, 2010, pp. 59–60.

Bratta, Phil and Malea Powell. "Introduction to the Special Issue: Entering the Cultural Rhetorics Conversations." *Enculturation*, 2016, http://enculturation.net/entering-the-cultural-rhetorics-conversations.

Brennan-Horley, Chris and Chris Gibson. "Where Is Creativity in the City? Integrating Qualitative and GIS Methods." *Environment & Planning*, vol. 41, 2009, pp. 2595–614. *JSTOR*, doi: 10.1068/a41406.

Cameron, Deborah. *Working with Spoken Discourse*. Sage, 2005.

Clark-Kazak, Christina. "Ethical Considerations: Research with People in Situations of Forced Migration." *Refuge*, vol. 33, no. 2, 2017, pp. 11–7.

Cobos, Casie Gabriela Raquel Ríos, et al. "Interfacing Cultural Rhetorics: A History and a Call." *Rhetoric Review*, vol. 37, no. 2, 2018, pp. 139–54. doi: 10.1080/07350198.2018.1424470.

Cruz, Cindy. "Toward an Epistemology of a Brown Body." *International Journal of Qualitative Studies in Education*, vol. 14, no. 5, 2001, pp. 657–69.

Edbauer, Jenny. "Unframing Models of Public Distribution: From Rhetorical Situation to Rhetorical Ecologies." *Rhetoric Society Quarterly*, vol. 35, no. 4, 2005, pp. 5–24.

Flores, Lisa A. "Creating Discursive Space through a Rhetoric of Difference: Chicana Feminists Craft a Homeland." *Quarterly Journal of Speech*, vol. 82, no. 2, 1996, pp. 142–56, *Routledge*.

Glenn, Cheryl. "A Rhetorical Art for Resisting Discipline(s)." *JAC*, vol. 22, no. 2, 2002, pp. 261–91. https://www.jstor.org/stable/20866487.

Gruwell, Leigh. *Making Matters: Craft, Ethics, and New Materialist Rhetorics*. 1st ed. Utah State University Press, 2022.

Haraway, Donna. *Staying with the Trouble: Making Kin in the Chthulucene*. Duke UP, 2016.

Hesse-Biber, Sharlene, ed. *Feminist Research Practice: A Primer*. Sage, 2013.

Hesford, Wendy S. "Cosmopolitanism and the Geopolitics of Feminist Rhetoric." *Rhetorica in Motion: Feminist Rhetorical Methods and Methodologies*, edited by Eileen E. Schell and K. J. Rawson, University of Pittsburgh Press, 2010, pp. 53–70.

Hesford, Wendy S. and Eileen Schell. "Configurations of Transnationality: Locating Feminist Rhetorics." *College English*, vol. 70, no. 5, 2008, pp. 461–70. *JSTOR*, http://www.jstor.org/stable/25472283.

Hidalgo, Alexandra, et al. "Listening to Stories: Practicing Cultural Rhetorics Pedagogy." *Constellations*, vol. 4, 2018. https://constell8cr.com/conversations/cultural-rhetorics-scholarship/.

Holland, Madeline. "Stories for Asylum: Narrative and Credibility in the United States' Political Asylum Application." *Refuge*, vol. 34, no. 2, 2018, pp. 85–93.

Inskeep, Steve. "A U.S. Border Shelter That Attracts Asylum Seekers Far and Wide." *Morning Edition*, NPR, 20 Mar. 2014, https://www.npr.org/sections/parallels/2014/03/20/291408051/a-u-s-border-shelter-that-attracts-asylum-seekers-far-and-wide.

Johnson, Ruth Laura. *Community-Based Qualitative Research: Approaches for Education and the Social Sciences*. Sage, 2017.

Leaning, Jennifer. "Ethics of Research in Refugee Populations." *The Lancet*, vol. 357, no. 9266, 2001, pp. 1432–3.

Licona, Adela C. "(B)orderlands' Rhetorics and Representations: The Transformative Potential of Feminist Third-Space Scholarship and Zines." *NWSA Journal*, vol. 17, no. 2, 2005, pp. 104–29. *JSTOR*, https://www.jstor.org/stable/4317128.

Loots, Gerrit, et al. "Practicing a Rhizomatic Perspective in Narrative Research." *Doing Narrative Research*, edited by Molly Andrews et al. SAGE Publications, 2013, pp. 108–25.

Lisle, Debbie. *The Global Politics of Contemporary Travel Writing*. Cambridge University Press, 2006.

McLees, Leslie. "A Postcolonial Approach to Urban Studies: Interviews, Mental Maps, and Photo Voices on the Urban Farms of Dar es Salaam, Tanzania." *The Professional Geographer*, vol. 65, no. 2, 2013, pp. 283–95, *EBSCO*.

Miller, Tina. "Doing Narrative Research? Thinking through the Narrative Process." *Feminist Narrative Research*, edited by Jo Woodiwiss et al. Oxford, 2017, pp. 39–63.

Moraga, Cherríe. "La Güera." *The Bridge Called My Back*, edited by Cherríe Moraga and Gloria Anzaldua. SUNY Press, 2015, pp. 22–9.

Refugee Studies Centre. "Ethical Guidelines for Good Research Practice." *Refugee Survey Quarterly*, vol. 26, no. 3, 2007, pp. 162–72.

Reyes, Monica and Andy Nájera. "Putting the Pieces Together: The Rhetoric of Oral Tradition in Early 20th Century Rio Grande Valley." *Supplemental Studies in Rio Grande Valley History*, edited by Milo Kearney et al. University of Texas, Rio Grande Valley, 2017, pp. 219–35.

Reynolds, Nedra. *Geographies of Writing: Inhabiting Places and Encountering Difference*. Southern Illinois UP, 2004.

Reynolds, Nedra. "Location: New Sites for Understanding Discursive Authority." *Rhetoric Review*, vol. 11, no. 2, 1993, pp. 325–38.

Rice, Jenny. "From Architectonic to Tectonics: Introducing Regional Rhetorics." *Rhetoric Society Quarterly*, vol. 42, no. 3, 2012, pp. 201–13. doi: 10.1080/02773945.2012.682831.

Rich, Adrienne. "Notes Toward a Politics of Location." *Blood, Bread, and Poetry: Selected Prose 1979-1985*. Norton, 1986, pp. 210–31.

Riley-Mukavetz, Andrea M. "Towards a Cultural Rhetorics Methodology: Making Research Matter with Multi-generational Women from the Little Traverse Bay Band." *Rhetoric, Professional Communication and Globalization*, vol. 5, no. 1, 2014, pp. 108–25.

Rose, Gillian. *Visual Methodologies: An Introduction to Researching with Visual Materials*. Sage, 2016.

Smith, Valerie J. "Ethical and Effective Ethnographic Research Methods: A Case Study with Afghan Refugees in California." *Journal of Empirical Research on Human Research Ethics*, vol. 4, no. 3, 2009, pp. 59–72.

Zepeda, Candace. "Chicana Feminism." *Decolonizing Rhetoric & Composition Studies*, edited by Iris D. Ruiz and Raul Sánchez, Palgrave Macmillan, 2019, pp. 137–51.

3 *En la Frontera*

Resisting Spatial Conventions

This chapter explores how "space/place influences, constrains, enables, and constitutes various types of rhetorical activity" for people who seek asylum (Senda-Cook et al. 103). I especially look at spaces and places of two distinct, yet overlapping rhetorical ecologies: the U.S. asylum system and the Rio Grande Valley (RGV) where the shelter is located. By weaving together stories about the spatial rhetorics of both the U.S. asylum process and the RGV, I demonstrate how LPP's positioning in the RGV has fostered its formation as a Third Space, aligning with Edbauer who posits that "exigence is more like a shorthand way of describing a series of events," rather than one discreet cause located in a contained rhetorical situation (8).

In order to explore the rhetoricity of the concepts of space and place more richly, I first define important terms and ideas. Next, I conceptualize space and place through describing how spaces like airports, border patrol holding cells, or detention centers perpetuate the belief that people who seek asylum at national borders are criminals engaging in illegal behavior through their movement and request for safety. I demonstrate how the RGV uses space-based advocacy initiatives to destabilize the ideology that people who seek asylum are criminals. Such a discussion is important because the RGV's experience with negotiating fixed labels and agency through spatial positioning has created long-lasting wounds, hope, and intuited knowledge about border life for those who embody the area.

Space, Place, and Labels of Criminalization

Like rhetoricians Samantha Senda-Cook, Micheal K. Middleton, and Danielle Endres, I borrow from cultural geographers Greg Dickinson, Carole Blair, and Brian L. Ott who see space and place as interconnected, equally meaningful entities, with place being a more specific location associated with a relative, yet general space. For example, public and private—those loose conceptions—are applied to spaces. The places associated with those respective spaces may be the Louvre Museum in Paris or the kitchen in a friend's apartment.

DOI: 10.4324/9781003349693-3

Conceptualizing space is important because it helps us understand what conventions or routines of meaning-making happen there, or as Endres and Senda-Cook explain, "space refers to a more general notion of how society and social practices are regulated (and sometimes disciplined) by spatial thinking (e.g., capitalist mode of production or gendered notions of public and private space)" (259–60). In fact, cultural geographers understand that material location, discourse, and bodies work together to enact "a normatively governed scenery (and associated storylines), which cite certain subject positions as obvious and legitimate ways to be and act" (Hulton and Introna 1366). In other words, we use our location as part of our rhetorical assemblage to make meaning, especially when we rely on established norms about what sorts of messages can be made in certain spaces. By understanding the ways in which people make meaning in spaces, on a broad scale, we are able to study how such rhetorics manifest—and, just as importantly, resist—spatial rhetorical norms in specific places. Thus, a place—"semi-bounded," "material," "embodied," and "particular" (Endres and Senda-Cook 259)—can be perceived as an "instantiation of spatial practices" (Senda-Cook et al. 97).

As I consider how the embodiment of certain places creates problematic labels for displaced people, I agree with rhetorician Katrina Powell's assertion that "the shifting of an identity is arguably violent. That is to say, displacement is a jolt to one's sense of self—a jolt to one's identity" (Powell, "Constructing Identities" 301). I argue that part of this violence and pain stems from the fixed labels of displacement ("migrant," "refugee," "illegal immigrant," or "asylum-seeker") that are thrust upon people (through U.S. immigration policies, media, or host communities) who mobilize across geopolitical borders because often these labels are associated with illegal movement.

The labels, while defined in a variety of ways by a variety of groups, may all have connotations of criminality, depending on the host communities they seek to enter. For example, Alissa R. Ackerman and Rich Furman describe how laws work to strategically target undocumented immigrant's everyday life as "illegal"; it is a felony, for instance, for undocumented immigrants (in some U.S. states like Arizona) to even seek to obtain a driver's license. In this way, "immigrants are more likely to be arrested and detained for facts that have not been traditionally viewed as illegal" (Ackerman and Furman 254). Connotations of criminality are especially relevant when considering the labels immigrants bear within the rhetorical ecology of the U.S. asylum system because *where someone is located when they ask for international protection from persecution* affords certain labels—according to U.S. immigration policies—and provides access to (or denial of) certain rights. Such labels and policies then play a part in how displaced people identify or are identified by others.

Perhaps the most familiar terms heard in the U.S. are "refugee" and "asylum-seeker." These terms are commonly used interchangeably because both labels reference people who have had to flee their country because they have "a well-founded fear of persecution for reasons of race, religion, nationality, political opinion or membership in a particular social group" (United Nations High Commission on Refugees 14; I-589 Instructions 2). "Asylum" is sought by those who, for any variety of reasons, have not yet processed their claim to remain in a safe country through the United Nations prior to arriving either within or outside an official port of entry. For this reason, people seeking asylum (again, according to U.S. immigration policies) may also be unofficially referred to as prima facie refugees. What is important for me to make clear about the "asylum-seeker" label is that it problematically creates "spatially differentiated subjects with distinctive rights" (Gorman 38). This spatial differentiation significantly affects how the nation-state is able to normalize oppressive policies which impact the spaces, mobility, and perceptions of displaced people as "criminal" (Ackerman and Forman; Coleman and Kocher; Dauvergne).

Gillian McFadyen argues a complex idea, informed by Jacques Derrida's concept of "hostipitality" about such labels and how a combination of hostility and hospitality is played out in the asylum system through the theory of labeling. In *Of Hospitality*, Jacques Derrida explains how unconditional hospitality does not exist as long as there are borders, windows, and doors, or "conditions" on who may enter. The term "hostipitality" refers to how marginalized people are excluded through conditions and are only welcomed if they are willing to forsake their otherness. Building off Derrida's ideas, McFadyen argues that "through labeling, there emerges a hierarchy that situates the label of refugee at the pinnacle, followed then by the label of asylum seeker, bogus asylum seeker, illegal immigrant and so on" (McFadyen, "Labelling," 603). Work by Sumana Chattopadhyay agrees with McFadyen about the problematic impact space-based labels have for displaced people:

> Refugees apply for permission to come to a country while they are still outside the host country. Refugees are often perceived as escaping persecutions in their native societies and are viewed with compassion. Asylum seekers, on the other hand, are more visible in that they [sometimes] show up at the border of the host country or even enter the country without papers and seek asylum, while staying within the borders of the host country. (Chattopadhyay 180)

As Allison Mountz describes, because of the ever-increasing policing and securing of borders, nation-states may be more inclined to offer protection to resettled refugees who have applied abroad prior to arriving, while also decreasing the number of individuals who traverse to make an asylum claim in person at a national border: "To inhibit this unscripted movement, governments have enhanced 'front end' enforcement practices to deter potential asylum-seekers from reaching sovereign territory to make a claim" ("Wait," 382). For example, "Migrant Protection Protocol" forces certain asylum applicants who have traveled by land, through Mexico, in route to the U.S. to remain in Mexico while their case is being processed in the U.S. (Burnett, "Changes"). Now commonly referred to simply as "Remain in Mexico," this policy was most likely impacted by the federal administration's frustration with both migrant "caravans" or large groups of people seeking asylum who travel together for safety so that they do not have to work with a human smuggler (Diao) and the scant construction of the promised border wall (Perez-Davis). The U.S. used other approaches to deter these caravans from traveling through Mexico. This included violent restrictions through border policing, which included deploying active National Guard soldiers to the RGV (which I personally saw overtake an abandoned furniture store as a post [also described in Findell]), as well as Mexican soldiers using tear gas on those seeking to travel north through their southern border (BBC News). This policy was a seemingly non-violent approach to offer an option known within migration policy as a "safe-third country," where people seeking international safety are allowed to live and work with some government benefits while they wait for their asylum claim to be processed in another country.

However, the Mexican *frontera* within the state of Tamaulipas that sits opposite the RGV is notoriously dangerous, even receiving the same high-level warning of threat risk as Afghanistan, Iraq, Syria, Somalia, North Korea, and Yemen from the U.S. State Department due to intensely embedded corruption of organized crime from *Las Zetas*, one of the offspring of the far-reaching Gulf Cartel which operate with extreme effectiveness in many facets of daily life in Mexico. In fact, within ten months of the policy being enacted, there were roughly 340 cases of violence, kidnapping, or torture confirmed which targeted people seeking asylum within Mexico (Human Rights First). The Migration Policy Institute has also offered a critique of "Remain in Mexico," especially offering previous examples as warnings that "[the] reality is that these arrangements have generally proven to be difficult to enforce, have played little role in deterring new claims, and have added new complexities to procedures for already overwhelmed asylum systems." Particularly troubling is how such a policy may only encourage border crossings which rely on human smugglers and the dangers such smugglers pose. Migrant Protection Protocols are just one example of the problematic "hierarchy" of labels for displaced individuals and the socially constructed perspectives about their credibility and rights to seek international safety. Most importantly for this chapter, such policies demonstrate how the nation-state uses space/place to reify the ideology that people who seek asylum at a national border are criminals.

"To Follow the Process Is to Be in Prison": Spaces in the U.S. Asylum System

The LPP clients I spoke to helped me conceptualize how spaces work as a means to criminalize people seeking asylum. The spaces and their associated rhetorical affordances and constraints were diverse; however, I focus here on ports of entry, and of course, sites of incarceration, like border patrol holding cells or detention centers. LPP clients described how they experienced space by assembling their material location, often resulting in clients' criminalization by policed borders and containment.

Policed Borders

As someone flees to a safe country, they encounter policed borders which alter their ability to move, plan, or control their own trajectories; this lack of control about how they are able to remain or move is attributed to how their movements are interpreted as criminal. Issa's story exemplifies this well. After she and her family endured extreme violence because of her political beliefs, Issa decided to run for her life, crossing undetected into a neighboring country in Africa for help. Her only plan was to take refuge there, but when this country refused to allow her to stay and instead offered her assistance (including a fake passport and plane ticket) to get to Europe, she had no choice but to accept a drastic change of plans and location. She was directed to dispose of the passport as soon as she landed, especially before asking for asylum within the airport. The plan failed, and she was denied permission to enter the European country and put on a plane to Los Angeles instead.

Mountz explains how many like Issa experience such a fast-paced shift in their location and path with no room for inquiry about their international rights:

> Liminal spaces of enforcement include ambiguous locales such as stateless rooms in airports, dynamic zones of interdiction in the "hot spots" where smugglers operate and remote sites of detention within and beyond sovereign territory. In these thresholds between sovereign and non-sovereign territory, asylum-seekers face legal ambiguities.
>
> (Mountz 385)

Indeed, an airport, crammed with people bearing legal permission to move and remain, was a material contrast to the only authentic and material form of identification that Issa carried—her ID card for the political party resisting those in power in her home country. In other words, her identification card rhetorically assembled with the airport space (immigration officers; airport security; security software and databases) as a material proof of her exclusion both at home and within her current liminal space of a European airport. Her mobility was then interpreted as criminal and suspect, prompting border security and airport staff to deny her access to the country.

Issa's experience demonstrates how nation-states within "the Global North work marginal times and places to their advantage" to deny mobility to those needing refuge (Mountz, "Wait," 387). As Mountz explains, scrutinizing "the geography of exclusion in sites between states reveals not only the particular arrangements that structure limbo, but also the distinct outcomes" of displaced people's paths ("Wait," 391). For example, Santos, from the Caribbean, describes how when he first presented himself at a port of entry in the southwest U.S., Customs and Border Protection (CBP) agents told him to "go back. We don't want anymore immigrants." Even though Santos presented himself at a U.S. designated "port of entry," his denial to enter is most likely connected to the "Presidential Proclamation Addressing Mass Migration Through the Southern Border of the United States." Otherwise known as "The Asylum Ban," this federal policy claimed that denying those who entered the country outside of "ports of entry" was based on the President's authority to bar any immigrant who may be dangerous to the United States (Horsley and Gonzalez). The policy was challenged in court by the American Civil Liberties Union, the Center for Constitutional Rights, and the Southern Poverty Law Center shortly after it was enacted. Among other concerns, the policy undermines both international and domestic law which clearly protects someone's right to claim asylum whether they entered the country at or outside a designated port of entry (UNHCR, "Convention," 5).

Additionally, this legislation demonstrated that people seeking asylum were labeled as both criminals and "dangerous," further adding to their alienation. After being denied entry, Santos returned the following day to try again, and he described that he felt "empowered" because he knew his rights as a "citizen of the world." Despite his confidence in his rights to claim asylum in the U.S., he was told directly by the chief CBP officer on duty, "you're going to be imprisoned, and only God knows how long you would be there." The ambiguity in Santos and Issa's entrance and denial into countries demonstrates how the people who seek asylum by traversing to borders are interpreted as a criminal act despite, as Santos correctly understood, it is a right they possess.

Containment

In addition to policed borders, clients who had experienced spaces of incarceration as part of the asylum process detailed how the materiality of their detainment worked to criminalize them as asylum-seekers or immigrants. If entering through a U.S. CPB port of entry, a person seeking asylum is then detained in holding cells at CPB facilities, commonly known as "*la hielera*," the Spanish word for freezer or icebox, due to its cold temperatures. Within this time, participants who experienced these cells described how they did not have access to adequate medical attention; this lack of care resulted in the death of several immigrants, including two children, 7-year-old Jakelin Caal and 8-year-old Felipe Gomez-Alonza in 2018 (Miroff; Stewart). Santos described the material conditions of the holding cell where he spent four days:

> No shower, no washing your mouth, no—only in a small room that we call the freezer, in Spanish is "*la hielera*" because it is too cold. They do

> it on purpose, I don't know why. Maybe a small room like this. I mean 2 meters by 2 meters. They keep there maybe 20 to 30 immigrants sleeping on the floor, covering themselves with only with a sheet of, like, aluminum paper—this very thin—that you see on the movies, well—that wasn't a movie, that was real life. I stayed there 4 days. After that, they opened the door, they said, you, you, you, you and you, pick up all of your S, H, that you leaving this place. Where are we going to? You don't care. It's not your problem. Okay. So they took me to Southwest U.S. [detention facility].

The treatment that Santos describes within the holding cell demonstrates he had been deprived of human dignity within this interstitial place. By not allowing people in the holding cells access to adequate health care, reasonable amounts of personal space, a bed, or opportunities for personal hygiene, the nation-state is able to materially identify them as "included through exclusion" and also "resubjectified as groups," a mass, a surge, a flow of outsiders and illegals (Mountz, "Wait," 386). This is seen in Santos' description of the mass of bodies being held together without care. People seeking asylum are then denied access by being labeled as criminals: "Stripped of individual identities, they become, rather, a collective threat, which explains why they are there [incarcerated or outside of national borders], safely at a distance from here" (Mountz, "Wait," 387). Santos' recollection of how he and his counterparts were not called by name, but rather simply labeled as "you, you, you, you and you," emphasizes how collective bodies, not as individuals, but as homogenized, impersonal, and nameless subjects, are kept in groups in order to counter any individual worth that their lives and stories have.

The same CPB holding cells are the spaces where the most notorious of the U.S. executive branch's immigration policies took place: "Zero Tolerance," which officially began on May 7, 2018, but had been in effect for much longer than that (Hennessy-Fiske). An extension of the "Asylum Ban," this policy directed the arrest and prosecution of any person caught crossing the U.S. southwest border outside of a "port of entry," even those seeking asylum. For families who crossed together, this meant that children were separated from their adult family members or caregivers while the latter were in federal jails (Burnett, "Curb"; Miller, "Separations"). These children were often sent to foster homes or shelters under the Department of Health and Human Services; however, reports indicate that government efforts to reunite families were insufficient and ineffective (Lind). The public outcry against this policy and those who enforced it, such as former Secretary of Homeland Security Kirstjen Nielsen who oversaw this policy during her tenure, was swift and intense (from a variety of groups, such as the American Academy of Pediatrics, the American College of Physicians, and the American Psychiatric Association, to name a few), eventually leading to the policy's termination in June of the same year. Suffice it to say, the irreparable and multi-layered damage that has been done to families who suffered from this policy is far-reaching and devastating. "Zero Tolerance" was another material way that the federal administration sought to criminalize people seeking asylum through using space (through confinement and physical separation from their families) to dehumanize and depersonalize them for seeking safety.

After a few days, and being processed at CBP, Santos was sent to an immigration detention center; these spaces are often located in deep rural areas where lawyers are scarce (Mountz, *Seeking Asylum*, 107). In addition, many of these detention centers are privately owned, and despite being under government contracts, media have reported the scant oversight the government maintains over these centers. These privately owned centers have reportedly maintained inhumane conditions, especially regarding access to health care (Ackerman and Furman; Leaños, "Private") and proper nutrition. Detention centers are another material space which positions displaced people as criminals. Santos describes the material conditions of detention explicitly:

> So I stayed in Southwest U.S. [detention facility] 12 days. Many officers there, they were saying, like "you are immigrant, like you are nothing, you are garbage, you don't deserve to be here. This is my country. We don't want you here." I mean from 100 officers, maybe 1 or 2 were nice or just normal. And I don't know why, but always the—the nicer ones, they look like white, blonde, blue eyes. But the bad officers always look like descendant [sic] of immigrants too. I don't know, maybe Mexico, South America, Central America, who knows? But anyway, I was there, I had to follow the process.

Indeed, Santos' experience in detention exemplifies how the power of the nation-state attempts to materially crystallize its own homogeneous identity; this is examined widely in Judith Butler and Gayatri Chakravorty Spivak's *Who Sings the Nation State?* Most notably, Butler and Spivak observe how statelessness is the result of such policies that many federal administrations have enforced which normalize "states of exception" that subvert international rights, even at the expense of the nation-state's founding values (35). Similarly, in her discussion of how nations in the Global North use the term, "illegal," as seen in the detention officer's labeling of Santos as "nothing," "garbage," and not deserving to be in the U.S., Dauvergne explains how policies such as detaining migrants are meant to show strength, but this is not "sovereignty transformed by globalizing forces … not a sovereignty ebbing away to the benefit of all concerned …, but simple traditional territorial sovereignty controlling them in place" (91).

The result of this spatial control also illustrates how "[in] order for inclusion within the nation to increase, the exclusion of the other against which the nation is imagined must also increase" (Dauvergne 95). Santos shows that he internalizes this exclusion because of his location ("I was there, I had to follow the process"), despite the fact that many officers who berated him seemed to be immigrants or descendants of immigrants themselves. Through his positioning in the facility, Santos understood that as an immigrant, he had little choice but to endure his criminalization. Santos sums up the experience in detention as he carried the label of "immigrant" as he says, "it is the same to call detention a prison … the only thing that is different is that you are an immigrant and not a national criminal" (Santos).

Santos describes his experience with the asylum process simply: "To follow the process is to be in prison." In other words, Santos interprets that the official path to refuge in the U.S. for someone seeking asylum is to be physically located in ("be in") spaces which position him as a criminal. To add to this, the frustrations and trials which many, like Santos, endured are exacerbated by their spatial positioning and how those positionings mark them as "illegal" not simply to the country in which they seek refuge but to any nation (Dauvergne 84; Ackerman and Furman 253). While being "illegal" is often read negatively in and of itself, Dauvergne argues that the word is more dangerous in that it is "empty of content. It says even less than other identity slots in the migration hierarchy … It circumscribes identity solely in terms of a relationship with law: those who are illegal have broken (our) law" (Dauvergne 92–3).

And as the identities of those who seek asylum are reduced and homogenized, readers and viewers, usually within the Global North, are free to imbue those identities "with any attributes we desire" (Dauvergne 93), such as rapists, terrorists, and drug dealers. Mountz echoes such points, as she argues how "[geography] and the law are intertwined in many ways, and legal identities of migrants take shape through the production of particular geographies. Legal identities of those 'at sea' or 'detained abroad' correspond with an assumption about who 'they' are" (Mountz, *Seeking Asylum*, xviii). Such an insight from critical refugee studies overlaps with rhetorician Nedra Reynolds' position on how where a person comes from dictates what places and paths they are allowed to access (Geographies 11).

The Rio Grande Valley

Thus far, I have shared client stories about spaces that detain and criminalize people seeking asylum. These spaces are webbed in the rhetorical ecology of the U.S. asylum system. In this section, I explore how, as a specific place and rhetorical ecology that sits along the U.S.-Mexico border, the RGV (where LPP is located) relies on its enduring experience with immigration policies, xenophobia, and cultural ambiguity to cultivate alternatives to the conventional uses of space which work to delineate lines of difference. Thus, people seeking asylum who inhabit the RGV may experience the support of advocacy groups who resist the fixed label of people seeking asylum as "criminal."

Border Wounds

As noted in Chapter 1, the majority of people seeking asylum in the U.S. enter through the RGV in south Texas. The RGV, the specific place where LPP is located, is 86% Hispanic and sits on the southernmost tip of Texas along the Rio Grande River, a geographical boundary between Mexico and the U.S. The RGV consists of four counties and is one of the fastest growing yet most impoverished areas of the U.S.; for example, in the cities of McAllen and my hometown of Brownsville, 21% and 26.5% of people live in poverty, respectively ("Brownsville, Texas"). A long history of border policing, strife, cross-cultural relations, and socioeconomic struggle makes this area known for the painful ambiguity and demarcation of identities associated with border life; this liminality is especially heightened for displaced individuals who need to hide or keep moving in order to survive.

A pioneering and enduring voice of the RGV is cultural rhetorician and Chicana feminist, Gloria Anzaldúa, who writes about the (im)mobility perpetuated by both ambiguity and distinctions of national, cultural, and linguistic identity. In her watershed work, *Borderlands/La Frontera: The New Mestiza*, she describes her experiences growing up in the RGV by describing the place as a "vague and undetermined place created by the emotional residue of an unnatural boundary … in a constant state of transition" (Anzaldúa 25). While Anzaldúa writes specifically about Chicanx experiences with located identity on the southwest U.S. border, she qualifies her perspectives by stating how "the psychological borderlands … are not particular to the Southwest" (19), and all "psyches resemble the bordertowns" making the conflict internal yet "played out in outer terrains" (109). In other words, people seeking asylum may profoundly identify with Chicana feminist concepts which articulate the plural, non-binary, contradictory, and ambiguous identities that come from "a struggle of flesh, a struggle of borders, an inner war" (Anzaldúa 100).

As a place, Anzaldúa underscores how the stark dualism of the RGV is attributed to its location on a national border; thus, the RGV, as a particular place, is conceptualized in terms of a border, a more general space. For Anzaldúa, the RGV is unique in that it is policed, so it is best described as a "thin edge of/barbed wire" (25) and a "1,950 mile-long open wound" (24), impacting how people move, hide, and settle across the U.S. borderlands. Because the RGV consistently sees the highest clandestine crossings of immigrants, including people seeking asylum, this border is painful in that it clearly delineates an "'us' and 'them' line, so familiarly drawn to constitute the nation" (Dauvergne 90). Mathew Coleman and Austin Kocher also describe how the U.S.-Mexico border "has emerged as exceptional in relation to homeland security and the national security threats posed by unauthorized entry" (228) because, as Dauvergne describes, migration laws are paramount to formulating how we read individuals at border sites, like the RGV (85).

For those who settle here, Anzaldúa describes how the RGV is "not a comfortable territory to live in, this place of contradictions. Hatred, anger and exploitation are the prominent features of this landscape" (19). However, the RGV is one of the easiest landscapes to navigate for human smugglers or *coyotes* who are hired by immigrants who try to cross the border undetected because the RGV is geographically closer to the border than other crossing points in California. Additionally, much of the area is privately owned or protected by wildlife refuge and federal laws, making active policing difficult for CBP. Clearly, the labels associated with the RGV are based on this movement, namely, "*[l]os atrevasados* … those who cross over" (25) and "the wetback" (33).

Anzaldúa describes "*[l]os atrevasados*" as "those who cross over, pass over, or go through the confines of the 'normal' (25) because 'the only legitimate' inhabitants are those in power, the whites and those who align themselves with whites" (25–6). While Anzaldúa writes mostly about Chicanx communities, her experiences clearly mirror the pushback to the arrival of people seeking asylum through the RGV. For example, another shelter community in the RGV (similar to LPP) recently faced opposition from the locals because of the attempt to relocate their facility to meet the increasing demands for more space for clients and volunteers. The new facility was based in the town center, and neighborhood residents strongly opposed it during city commission meetings because they perceived the people seeking asylum as "unsafe," causing the city government to order the shelter to vacate the premises in 90 days (Ferman). The neighborhood residents' feelings were no doubt linked to the discourses of criminality and danger which surround people who seek asylum; it is no wonder that the neighborhood residents were uneasy with displaced people residing in their area when spaces like detention centers and walls are the spaces commonly associated with people seeking asylum.

Also reflecting Anzaldúa's point about how power and ethnicity mix to legitimize mobility and identity is the proliferation of private-run detention facilities in the RGV. These facilities are seen as a boon to the poverty-stricken rural areas wherein they operate within the RGV because they generate billions of dollars for the local economy. When these facilities are rightfully shut down due to health and safety violations, the local community often faces devastating economic loss in an already impoverished setting.

In fact, the RGV is reopening the infamous "Ritmo" facility (which would now be solely used for migrant detainees) because locals are in need of jobs (Reigstad). The nickname, "Ritmo," likens the facility to Guantanamo Bay (a combination of Raymondville and Gitmo). The conditions that detainees reportedly faced during its operation are appalling and detailed by Erica B. Schrommer. Of the myriad of abuses, detainees claimed the guards had raped and sexually abused detainees as well as smuggled drugs within the center. Detainees eventually burned it down themselves in 2015.

Additionally, the "wetback" label refers to any immigrant who enters the U.S. through the river or other clandestine means, and this person is paradoxically vilified and preyed upon in ways that may be more hidden: "the *mojados* … float on inflatable rafts across *el rio Grande*, or wade or swim across, clutching their clothes over their heads. Holding onto the grass, they pull themselves along the banks with a prayer" (Anzaldúa 33), often facing rape or exploitation (Anzaldúa 25). Esther and Ayana, two participants from Central America, spoke about such vulnerabilities along the *frontera*. Esther expressed how swimming across the Rio Grande River (Figure 3.1) was so traumatic that she cannot clearly recall what happened to her afterward, but she remembers hallucinating as she was processed by CBP agents. Ayana, who also crossed the border clandestinely, was raped by a man while she hid from CBP agents along a heavily wooded area where U.S. ranches and private property often limit how CBP can operate. Her rape and the ongoing pain from that experience reflect Anzaldúa's points about how "*[l]a mojada, la mujer indocumentada*, is doubly threatened in this country. Not only does she have to contend with sexual violence, but also like all women, she is prey to a sense of physical helplessness. As a refugee, she leaves the familiar and safe home-ground to venture into the unknown and possibly dangerous terrain" (35).

Such labels, "*[l]os atrevasados*" or "wetback" commonly used in the RGV, coincide with the oppressive space-based labels that criminalize people seeking asylum. What is more, these labels not only connote criminality,

Figure 3.1 "The Rio Grande River" captures an on-the-ground view of the river and the surrounding brush on both the U.S. and Mexico sides. Photo by author.

but they also reference the dangerous and exploitive spatial positioning that displaced people in the RGV have endured (rivers, detention centers, or unsecured wooded areas) in their attempt to seek refuge.

When we study general spaces of control in asylum contexts, like borders, we observe how specific places, like the RGV, may push back against those spatially defined conventions and labels associated with criminality. Reynolds argues, for example, that "[the] more that spaces are 'controlled,' the more likely that new uses or practices develop as forms of resistance to order and control" (Reynolds, *Geographies*, 17). Additionally, while displacement may be faultily represented as a linear journey based on loss, (illegal) movement, and resettlement, Powell argues that people who are displaced "end up inhabiting a figurative 'third space' or 'hybrid identity'" which resists a "fixed identity" or label and instead demonstrates that "identity formation is a process rather than an outcome" (Powell, "Constructing Identities," 300). Such an argument is foundational for Chicana feminists who grapple with fixed labels, especially in the context of displacement and borders.

I contend, like Chicana feminists (and perhaps many who live in the RGV as well), that borders are unable to tightly sustain clear dualities, as they are messy, complex, and often contain material and ideological holes, leaving room for inclusion, connection, synthesis, and advocacy (Figure 3.2).

Figure 3.2 "Unfinished Border Fencing" shows a lonely stretch of border fencing along a dirt path. Photo by author.

Breaks in the Wall

The RGV, like all places, is not sealed: "Places, whether textual, material, or imaginary, are constructed and reproduced not simply by boundaries but also by practices [and] structures of feeling" (Reynolds, *Geographies*, 2). Reynolds, for example, argues how places, like the RGV, may be difficult to describe because they are "elusive and embodied" and "also contain embedded histories that aren't necessarily 'seen' but rather 'felt'" (146–7), as described in Anzaldúa's embodied perspectives of the RGV in Borderlands. Edbauer extends this point by arguing that places may "obtain their descriptions as good/bad sites from the affective and embodied experiences that circulate: feelings of fear or comfort, for instance" (Edbauer 11). Reynolds also explains how such feelings culminate from our lived experiences related to material conditions, objects, and geographies, which may very well subvert what is happening or present within the more general space. Anzaldúa, for example, muses on how her lived experiences inform her description of the RGV during a return visit:

> I still feel the old despair when I look at the unpainted, dilapidated, scrap lumber houses consisting mostly of corrugated aluminum. Some of the poorest people in the U.S. live in the Lower Rio Grande Valley, an arid and semi-arid land of irrigated farming, intense sunlight and heat, citrus groves next to chaparral and cactus. I walk through the elementary school I attended so long ago, that remained segregated until recently. I remember how the white teachers used to punish us for being Mexican. How I love this tragic valley of South Texas …
>
> (Anzaldúa 111–2)

As a felt site, and by locating her position in a more specific place, Anzaldúa is able to revise her conventional reaction, as a Chicana, to such a harsh space of an international border. In this way, the RGV affords a new consciousness that embraces plurality and is able to "break down the subject-object duality that keeps [someone] a prisoner" (102). This new consciousness, or a "mestiza consciousness," is developed in spaces which are transient, characterized by geographical, spiritual, linguistic, and cultural movement (Anzaldúa 36). The RGV is able to foster such a consciousness because it is problematic to attempt to meet stark demands for national, linguistic, and cultural identity within this particular place with such an overwhelming Chicanx population. Reynolds echoes such perspectives as she argues how borders are like discourse communities, and how "outsiders have to find a way in that imitates insider discourse … even if they then proceed to introduce a 'hybrid' discourse" and these breaks in the border allow for movement, exchange, ambiguity, and "change," even "if only briefly … or small" (*Geographies* 37). Although the movement may be painful for many, the truth is that most people in the RGV trace their roots in "crossing over," and while the demand for lines of difference may be common, the blurring of such lines is part of daily life.

Resisting Fixed Labels in the Rio Grande Valley through Advocacy

The RGV, as a "felt site" (Reynolds; Edbauer), has a long-standing history of pain, oppression, systematic racism, and negotiated agency (Anzaldúa 112). I argue that such a history makes the RGV a seasoned place for the collaborative construction of a Third Space, where people seeking asylum, often represented as "the squint-eyed, the perverse, the queer, the troublesome, the mongrel, the mulato, the half-breed, the half-dead" who "cross over" (Anzaldúa 25), may be able to form a supportive site of alliance which operates by shifting "from other-defined to self-defined" (Flores 152), thus resisting hegemonic labels centered on criminalization (Zepeda 142). Or as Tim Cresswell puts it, "the qualities of place that make them good strategic tools of power simultaneously make them ripe for resistance in highly visible and often outrageous ways" (164). As explained in Chapter 2, Third Space scholars understand that as people locate themselves within their physical surroundings and assemble materially with other bodies and things, there are opportunities for resistance and agency.

The agency that has the potential to exist within these in-between spaces demonstrates Pérez's view of how Third Space allows marginalized people room for "critique" of "what has been, what is, and what many of us hope will be. All at once [those in Third Space] live the past, present, and future" (Pérez 127). In addition, shelters like LPP have the possibility to generate what Anzaldúa would call "*una cultura mestiza*" (44) or a culture of daily practices where individuals choose to self-define, or forge their own identity through creating their own space, described as "a ground to stand on, a ground from which to view the world—a perspective" (44, 45). In Third Spaces, like the RGV, ambiguity is welcomed, and labels are problematic, as the inhabitants identify as complex and hybrid individuals.

Perhaps *una cultura mestiza* is most clearly seen in the local advocacy work for people seeking asylum in the RGV that is currently generating more attention and following. In addition to the emergency shelters (respite centers) in the RGV that have received national attention and praise for the overwhelming work involved in caring for people seeking asylum (Leaños, "Shelters"), there are also initiatives that take advantage of the between spaces of the RGV, like bridges and walls.

"Angry Tías and Abuelas," which won the Robert F. Kennedy Human Rights Award in the summer of 2019 for their service, and "Team Brownsville" are two separate organizations that began during the "Asylum Ban" policy in the summer of 2018 as a reaction to the conditions many people seeking asylum faced waiting for days on the Mexico-U.S. bridges because of the "Remain in Mexico" policy. Since then, these groups have fed thousands of people waiting on international bridges, offered financial and legal assistance, and even began a "sidewalk school" on the bridge itself, "Escuelita de la Banqueta" which conducts mini-lessons for all ages in reading, math, and geography. By locating the bulk of their respective work with people seeking asylum on the bridge, these organizations are material examples of how the RGV possesses unique affordances to blur fixed labels and cultivate ambiguity instead. Whereas these in-between spaces are often associated with distinct binaries of insider and outsider, such groups formulate opportunities for inclusion and resistance to conventional labels centered on criminalization.

Senda-Cook et al. have argued how "material changes" within a place (such as the sidewalk school on an international bridge) can lead to a reshaping of rhetorics associated with that particular place: "While these are often temporary reconstructions, by engaging in deliberate, long-term, and repeated efforts to materially reconstruct … places, such places can be invested with new meanings and reshaped to invite new practices" (Senda-Cook et al. 104). In other words, it is not conventional to have a school on an international bridge because it is for passing through and policing those who cross, not settling. In fact, organizations like "Angry Tías and Abuelas" have helped connect people seeking asylum who wait on the bridge every day with lawyers who will meet to discuss their case on the bridge itself. Such a practice demonstrates Third Space in that the people have created their own normalcy within a place that upends the spatial conventions; how they use the space and identify within the space is complicated and subverted.

Yet another example is the advocacy work from a local dragtavist (a drag queen who uses drag performance to promote social activism). Beatrix Lestrange, who has worked with LPP as a host for a "Bling-o" fundraiser event (Bingo with jewelry prizes), uses drag to call attention to the ways that identity is queer and shifting for all, including people seeking asylum and migrants who rely on international movements to forge a life of safety and dignity. In 2019, Lestrange and fellow native RGV dragtavists held an event at the border wall in my hometown of Brownsville, Texas to protest the ongoing construction that often cuts across the geographical landscape (Leaños, "Dragtavists"). In Lestrange's words, the protest aimed to "bring joy, positivity, beauty, drag, culture to whatever this [border wall] is" (qtd. in Leaños, "Drag Queens"). The dragtivists' revision and provision of a "culture" that they themselves have forged is based on their plurality of identity and a mixture of labels they bear, especially seen in Figure 3.3.

One dragtivist (second from right) dons a highly recognizable skirt, typically worn during *Charro* Days, the three-day festival held in my hometown of Brownsville, Texas and its Mexican sister city of Matamoros, Mexico. This festival celebrates the relations between the two nations as manifested in the diverse culture of the border space. Usually, people (in both cities) dress in

Figure 3.3 Dragtivists pose by the border wall in Brownsville, Texas. Photo by Reynaldo Leaños Jr. (Texas Public Radio). Used with permission.

traditional Mexican attire from the specific state where their ancestors are from. The particular dragtivist I reference wears a skirt signifying their connection to the Mexican state of Guanajuato. Such a performance subverts tradition, fixed identity, and conventional norms of space-based behavior particularly by employing traditional Mexican dress in drag performance within the U.S. to protest U.S. policies that involve Mexico. By assembling with the border wall as their backdrop and fellow performer, the dragtavists use the specific place to rhetorically resist the spatial conventions of an international bridge.

All of these advocacy efforts are shared by a diverse group of people, including white men and women within the RGV, as well as those who travel here to volunteer, mirroring Anzaldúa's sentiments about community service initiatives in the area:

> I think we need to allow whites to be our allies. Through literature, art, corridos, and folktales we must share our history with them so when they set up committees to help Big Mountain Navajos or the Chicano farmworkers or los Nicaragüenses they won't turn people away because of their racial fears and ignorances. They will come to see that they are not helping us but following our lead.
>
> (Anzaldúa 107)

Most of all, the advocacy efforts I describe here show how a place, like the RGV, is made and perpetuated not only through physical markers and boundaries but also through daily practices and the resulting feelings of those who dwell within them (de Certeau; Dobrin; Reynolds; Edbauer; Rice). As a place, RGV relies on "varying intensities of encounters and interactions—much like a weather system" (Edbauer 12) which bring about connections and contacts of people, events and ideas, moods and emotions (Edbauer 9–10). In other words, the RGV, as any place has the possibility to do, seizes the opportunity to resist spatial-identity conventions through revising how one behaves, feels, or identifies within the place.

Conclusion

The goal of this chapter was to locate LPP, within two distinct yet overlapping rhetorical ecologies of the RGV as well as the U.S. asylum system. I have shown how the "process" for refuge in the U.S. uses space/place to position people seeking asylum at a national border as criminals. People who desire to begin an asylum claim in this way must endure policed borders that may include physical violence, as well as detainment, or as Santos describes, "prison." I have also briefly discussed how the RGV, the southernmost border of the U.S., has generations of experience with negotiating fixed labels that work to homogenize people who have individual worth, stories, and experiences. Through local, grassroots advocacy work that upends spatial conventions, the native people in RGV have shared their intuition with people seeking asylum about how to foster "*una cultura mestiza*," or a way of life and perspective of the world that is built on self-defining and carving spaces of resistance through daily life (Anzaldúa 44, 45). Because of the shelter's location in the RGV, and the fact that many volunteers and staff are native to the area, it was important to notice the legacies and located knowledge that many people bring to the shelter every day in their volunteer and professional work.

In the following chapter, I demonstrate how as a Third Space, LPP is able to make room for agency specifically through the development of public narratives of credibility that may be expected from U.S. audiences on their own terms in their own time. Positioned as criminals by the U.S. asylum system, people seeking asylum are expected to defend themselves through an adversarial process where they must use compelling narratives to persuade the U.S. that they are in fear for their lives if they return to their home country. At LPP, however, clients are supported in their choices to make room for silence and listening, in order to tell stories grounded in mutual understanding instead of persuasion.

References

Ackerman, Alissa R. and Rich Furman. "The Criminalization of Immigration and the Privatization of the Immigration Detention: Implications for Justice." *Contemporary Justice Review*, vol. 16, no. 2, 2013, pp. 251–63. http://dx.doi.org/10.1080/10282580.2013.798506.

Anzaldúa, Gloria. *Borderlands/La Frontera: The New Mestiza*. Aunt Lute Books, 1987.

BBC News. "Migrant Caravan: Tear Gas on Guatemala Mexico Border." *BBC News*, 20 Oct. 2018, https://www.bbc.com/news/world-latin-america-45925186. Accessed 23 Oct. 2019.

Burnett, John. "To Curb Illegal Immigration, DHS Separating Families at The Border." *National Public Radio*, 27 Feb. 2018, https://www.npr.org/2018/02/27/589079243/activists-outraged-that-u-sborder-agents-separate-immigrant-families. Accessed 11 Oct. 2019.

Burnett, John. "Trump Administration Changes Border Policy to Discourage Asylum-Seekers." *National Public Radio*, 21 Dec. 2018, https://www.npr.org/2018/12/21/679057325/trump-administration-changesborder-policy-to-discourage-asylum-seekers. Accessed 11 Oct. 2019.

Butler, Judith and Gayatri Chakravorty Spivak. *Who Sings the Nation State?: Language, Politics, Belonging*. Seagull Books, 2007.

"Brownsville, Texas." *DataUSA*. 2021, https://datausa.io/profile/geo/brownsville-tx#:~:text=Poverty%20%26%20Diversity&text=26.5%25%20of%20the%20population%20for,the%20national%20average%20of%2012.6%25

Chattopadhyay, Sumana. "'You are Not Welcome Here!' Understanding News Coverage of Central American Migrant Families in Trump's America." *Journal of Family Communication*, vol. 19, no. 3, 2019, pp. 177–90, doi: 10.1080/15267431.2019.1632866.

Coleman, Mathew and Austin Kocher. "Detention, Deportation, Devolution and Immigrant Incapacitation in the US, post 9/11." *The Geographical Journal*, vol. 177, no. 3, 2011, pp. 228–37, doi: 10.1111/j.1475-4959.2011.00424.x.

Cresswell, Tim. *In Place/Out of Place: Geography, Ideology and Transgression*. University of Minnesota Press, 1996.

Dauvergne, Catherine. "Making People Illegal," *Critical Beings: Law, Nation and the Global Subject*, edited by Peter Fitzpatrick and Patricia Tuitt, Ashgate Publishing, 2004, pp. 83–99.

De Certeau, Michele. *The Practice of Everyday Life*. The University of California Press, 2011.

Derrida, Jacques. *Of Hospitality*. Stanford University Press, 2000.

Diao, Alexis. "Central American Migrants Arrive at U.S. Border to An Uncertain Future." *National Public Radio*, 29 Apr. 2019, https://www.npr.org/sections/thetwoway/2018/04/29/606890139/central-american-migrants-arrive-at-u-s-borderto-an-uncertain-future, Accessed 11 Oct. 2019.

Dobrin, Sidney I. "Writing Takes Place." *Ecocomposition: Theoretical and Pedagogical Approaches*, edited by Christian R. Weisser and Sidney I. Dobrin, State University of New York Press, 2001, pp. 11–25.

Edbauer, Jenny. "Unframing Models of Public Distribution: From Rhetorical Situation to Rhetorical Ecologies." *Rhetoric Society Quarterly*, vol. 35, no. 4, 2005, pp. 5–24.

Endres, Danielle and Samantha Senda-Cook. "Location Matters: The Rhetoric of Place in Protest." *Quarterly Journal of Speech*, vol. 97, no. 3, pp. 257–82, doi: 10.1080/00335630.2011.585167.

Ferman, Mitchell. "Mcallen Orders Catholic Charities to Vacate Immigrant Respite Center." *The McAllen Monitor*, 11 Feb. 2019, https://www.themonitor.com/2019/02/11/mcallen-orders-catholic-charitiesvacate-immigrant-respite-center/, Accessed 23 Oct. 2019.

Findell, Elizabeth. "Amid Growing Apprehensions at Border but No 'Caravan,' A Quiet Army Set to Depart Texas." *Statesmen*, 13 Dec. 2018, https://www.statesman.com/news/20181213/amid-growing-apprehensions-atborder-but-no-caravan-quiet-army-set-to-depart-texas, Accessed 23 Oct. 2019.

Gorman, Cynthia S. "Redefining Refugees: Interpretive Control and the Bordering Work of Legal Categorization in U.S. Asylum Law." *Political Geography*, vol. 58, no. 1, 2017, pp. 36–45. doi: http://dx.doi.org/10.1016/j.polgeo.2016.12.006.

Hennessy-Fiske, Molly. "U.S. Is Separating Immigrant Parents and Children To Discourage Others, Activists Say." *Los Angeles Times*, 20 Feb. 2018, https://www.latimes.com/nation/la-na-immigrant-family-separations-2018-story.html. Accessed 12 Oct. 2019.

Horsley, Scott and Richard Gonzalez. "Trump Administration Seeks to Limit Asylum Seekers with New Rule." *National Public Radio*, 8 Nov. 2018, https://www.npr.org/2018/11/08/665875770/trump-administration-seeks-tolimitasylum-seekers-with-new-rule. Accessed 11 Oct. 2019.

Hulton, Lotta and Lucas Introna. "On Receiving Asylum Seekers: Identity Working as a Process of Material-Discursive Interpellation." *Organization Studies*, vol. 40, no. 9, 2019, pp. 1361–86, *SAGE*.

Human Rights First. "Orders from Above: Massive Human Rights Abuses Under Trump Administration Return to Mexico Policy." *Human Rights First*, 2019, https://humanrightsfirst.org/library/orders-from-above-massive-human-rights-abuses-under-trump-administration-return-to-mexico-policy/h. Accessed 23 Oct. 2019.

"I-589, Application for Asylum and for Withholding from Removal: Instructions." *Department of Homeland Security U.S. Citizenship and Immigration Services*. https://www.uscis.gov/sites/default/files/files/form/i-589instr.pdf. Accessed 18 Jan. 2018.

Leaños, Reynaldo Jr. "A Private Prison Company with a Troubled Past Looks to Reopen an Immigration Detention Facility in Texas." *GBH*, 13 Jun. 2017, https://www.wgbh.org/news/2017-06-13/a-private-prison-company-with-a-troubled-past-looks-to-reopen-an-immigration-detention-facility-in-texash. Accessed 11 Oct. 2019.

Leaños, Reynaldo Jr. "Drag Queens Protest at Border Wall to Raise Money for LGBTQ Asylum Seekers." *NBC News*, 25 Feb. 2019, https://www.nbcnews.com/feature/nbc-out/drag-queens-protest-border-wall-raise-money-lgbtq-asylum-seekers-n975666h. Accessed 30 Apr. 2020.

Leaños, Reynaldo Jr. "Shelters and City Governments Scramble to Help Migrants in The Rio Grande Valley." *Texas Standard*, 7 Apr. 2019, https://www.texasstandard.org/stories/shelters-and-city-governments-scramble-to-help-migrants-in-the-rio-grande-valley/h. Accessed 11 Oct. 2019.

Lind, Dara. "It's Official: We'll Never Know the Real Scope of Trump's Family Separation Crisis." Vox, 17 Jan. 2019, https://www.vox.com/policy-andpolitics/2019/1/17/18186773/families-children-separated-trump-thousands. Accessed 16 Oct. 2019.

McFadyen, Gillian. "Memory, Language and Silence: Barriers to Refuge within the British Asylum System." *Journal of Immigrant & Refugee Studies*, 2018, pp. 1–17. *Sage*, doi: 10.1080/15562948.2018.1429697.

Miller, Michael. "Family Separations Could Double, Says Border Patrol Chief in Rio Grande Valley." *Washington Post*, 16 Jun. 2018, https://www.washingtonpost.com/local/family-separations-could-double-says-border-patrol-chief-in-rio-grande-valley/2018/06/16/13cdc042-70ee-11e8-bf86-a2351b5ece99_story.htmlh. Accessed 11 Oct. 2019.

Miroff, Nick. "Hours Before Her Collapse in U.S. Custody, a Dying Migrant Child's Condition Went Unnoticed." *Washington Post*, 14 Dec. 2018, https://www.washingtonpost.com/world/national-security/hours-before-her-collapse-in-us-custody-a-dying-migrant-childs-condition-went-unnoticed/2018/12/14/1c454d18-ffb8-11e8-862a-b6a6f3ce8199_story.htmlh. Accessed 11 Oct. 2019.

Mountz, Alison. *Seeking Asylum: Human Smuggling and Bureaucracy at the Border*. University of Minnesota Press, 2010.

Mountz, Alison. "Where Asylum-seekers Wait: Feminist Counter-topographies of Sites between States." *Gender, Place & Culture*, vol. 18, no. 3, 2011, pp. 381–99, doi: 10.1080/0966369X.2011.566370.

Pérez, Emma. *The Decolonial Imaginary: Writing Chicanas into History (Theories of Representation and Difference)*. Indiana University Press, 1999.

Perez-Davis, Leidy. "'Remain In Mexico' is Another Brick in Trump's Invisible Wall." *The Hill*, 16 Dec. 2018, https://thehill.com/opinion/immigration/421497-remain-in-mexico-is-another-brick-in-trumps-invisible-wall/h. Accessed 14 Oct. 2019.

Powell, Katrina M. "Rhetorics of Displacement: Constructing Identities in Forced Relocations." *College English*, vol. 74, no. 4, 2012, pp. 299–324.

Reigstad, Leif. "ICE Could Reopen an Infamous South Texas Detention Center." *Texas Monthly*, 27 Feb. 2017, https://www.texasmonthly.com/the-daily-post/ice-reopen-infamous-south-texas-detention-center/h. Accessed 23 Oct. 2019.

Reynolds, Nedra. *Geographies of Writing: Inhabiting Places and Encountering Difference*. Southern Illinois UP, 2004.

Rice, Jenny. "From Architectonic to Tectonics: Introducing Regional Rhetorics," *Rhetoric Society Quarterly*, vol. 42, no. 3, 2012, pp. 201–13.

Schrommer, Erica B. "After Years of Working With 'Ritmo' Detainees, I Know the Inhumane Facility Doesn't Deserve A Second Chance." *Texas Observer*, 10 Jul. 2018, https://www.texasobserver.org/after-years-of-working-with-ritmo-detainees-i-know-the-inhumane-facility-doesnt-deserve-a-second-chance/h. Accessed 23 Oct. 2019.

Senda-Cook, Samantha, Micheal K. Middleton, and Danielle Endres. "Rhetorical Cartographies: Mapping (Urban) Spaces." *Field Rhetoric: Ethnography, Ecology, and Engagement in the Places of Persuasion*, University of Alabama Press, 2018, pp. 95–119. *ProQuest Ebook Central*, http://ebookcentral.proquest.com/lib/unomaha/detail.action?docID=5492931.

Stewart, Ian. "Trump Blames Democrats for Deaths of Migrant Kids as DHS Secretary Visits Border." *National Public Radio*, 29 Dec. 2019, https://www.npr.org/2018/12/29/680932809/trump-blames-democrats-fordeaths-of-migrant-kids-as-dhs-secretary-visits-border. Accessed 12 Oct. 2019.

United Nations High Commission for Refugees (UNHCR). "Convention and Protocol Relating to the Status of Refugees." *UNHCR*, https://www.unhcr.org/us/media/convention-and-protocol-relating-status-refugeesh. Accessed 1 Nov. 2019.

Zepeda, Candace. "Chicana Feminism." *Decolonizing Rhetoric & Composition Studies*, edited by Iris D. Ruiz and Raul Sánchez, Palgrave Macmillan, 2016, pp. 137–51.

4 Public Narratives of Asylum and Silence as an Echo of Displacement

I met David shortly after he arrived in the U.S. He had only been at the shelter for a few days, and he was applying for asylum. His experiences had left him in great distress about sharing his story as part of his application. When considering how he would soon have to recount the persecution he faced, he admitted plainly, "I don't trust anyone; I don't know who to trust." Not only was he apprehensive about having to be vulnerable enough to tell the trauma he endured, but he also described confusion about having to piece together a story that would help him convince others of his fear to return home. He explains,

> I don't know really how am I feeling, but of course, I don't have maybe choice. If I had a choice, I couldn't show them this story. If I had another choice, if I had another choice, I shouldn't do it, but if there's no any other choice, I will just do it for maybe to help me if possible, to help me to get my family, which I am really very worried about how they live.
>
> (David)

I interpret David's reaction to composing a public narrative of asylum as focused on four primary inhibitions: lack of trust in his audience(s) ("I don't trust anyone; I don't know who to trust"); emotional trauma and disorientation ("I don't know really how am I feeling"); feelings of powerlessness in the asylum process ("I don't have maybe choice. If I had a choice, I couldn't show them this story"); and desperation for refuge ("I will just do it for maybe to help me if possible"). David helped me understand the desire to be silent, and his preference for silence is supported by previous scholarship concerning narratives of displacement as well as the staff and clients at LPP. Also, David's desire speaks to the rhetorical ecology of public narratives of asylum and the variety of constraints people seeking asylum face in simply initiating an application for asylum status.

This chapter highlights the unique storytelling challenges within the rhetorical ecology of the U.S. asylum system. Specifically, I share how the predominant ideology underpinning the narrative standards of the U.S. asylum

DOI: 10.4324/9781003349693-4

process is that persuasion and dominance are the goals of storytelling. Next, I share some stories from clients at LPP who thoughtfully resist public narratives and hegemonic representations of persecution through silence—a distinct shelter rhetoric. I argue that rather than demonstrate credible fear in ways that are easily recognizable to mainstream audiences in the Global North, clients' stories demonstrate what I describe as echoes of displacement, or narratives and silences which reflect traces of or reverberated responses to the trauma of persecution and dislocations of home. In this chapter, silence is an echo on which I exclusively focus.

The latter half of the chapter analyzes how as a Third Space within the rhetorical ecology of the U.S. asylum system, LPP listens to such echoes in order to offer rhetorical support for clients. Other echoes of displacement I observed, but are not discussed in this book are disordered narratives and numeration within narratives to tell their stories with dignity. The implication of this analysis is that LPP functions as a Third Space for people seeking asylum because it invites clients to share their stories on their own terms, not with the goal of domination, but with the intent of mutual understanding.

Credible Stories of Fear

After speaking with clients and staff, I adopted the term *public narratives of asylum* to emphasize the rhetorical ecology of asylum narrative production and how agencies of power, such as U.S. Citizenship and Immigration Services (UCIS), are implicated in the assemblage of certain kinds of stories. Indeed, "public narratives" is a term inspired by feminist narrative researcher Margaret R. Somers to describe how "narratives [are] attached to cultural and institutional formations larger than the single individual" (619).

Such ideas, of course, synthesize with rhetorical ecology scholars' perspective that "writers are ecological beings. Writers become a part of an environment; they are a product of that environment. They write themselves into the order of a system, and they help define that system" (Dobrin 19). Additionally, while narratives of asylum usually take place in officially confidential contexts, I describe them as "public" to emphasize how asylum narratives often require disclosing sensitive information and experiences to people, often strangers, who both influence and circulate such narratives in contexts within the larger rhetorical ecology such as courtrooms or law offices, which include a variety of listeners, like lawyers, judges, translators, interpreters, or volunteers.

By using a rhetorical ecology lens, I can appreciate how deeply interlinked public narratives of asylum are with the predominant, well circulated narrative norms often found in Western literature (Holland). There are several bureaucratic challenges and influences someone faces when sharing their story of persecution for asylum status, especially how narratives that are deemed credible usually adhere to Western narrative norms that contain certain key features, such as narrative consistency and recognizable characters and plotlines (Burki; Holland; Shuman and Bohmer; Vogl). In sum, the U.S. asylum system operates with the predominant ideology that an asylum applicant's narrative is credible if it is persuasive, and a persuasive narrative aligns with rigid Western literary storytelling standards.

Scholars have written about the intersection of rhetorics of displacement with human rights rhetorics (Powell, *Identity*) and human-interest portrayals in news media (Steimel, "Refugees"). An overlapping conclusion in these studies is that refugee narratives are based on stock characters; more specifically, Powell (174 *Identity*) contextualizes her discussion about the "narrative expectations of the displaced" (173) with Makau Mutua's work on human rights rhetorics' dependence on flat characterizations such as "savages," "victims," and "saviors" (Mutua 1). Indeed, such flat characterizations and plotlines, often stemming from "Western literary standards" (Holland 86), color what a narrative of sociopolitical escape is (Burki 6). What results, according to Madeline Holland's narrative scholarship, is a "conflation of literary storytelling and truthful storytelling in the context of asylum proceedings," and narratives which miss these standards may be read as inauthentic (Holland 86).

Another obstacle is the need for a person seeking asylum to tell their narrative chronologically and consistently across various tellings, or they may experience a barrier to gaining international protection (McFadyen 1; Vogl 73; Weaver et al. 82–3). In this obstacle, the challenge is more about how someone communicates their story, rather than the plot of the story itself. In fact, the client coordinator at LPP, Leticia, agrees with this scholarly observation, as she relays to clients every day how they must tell their stories in a "compelling way" in order to make their cases heard by lawyers and judges. A story that is told chronologically, for example, may represent "what a 'true story' sounds like" because it mirrors the "literary standards" audiences in the Global North know so well, highlighting how there is little "distinction between a true story and a story well told," making it difficult for us "to believe the stories of those who do not express their suffering 'well'" (Holland 91). Finally, a credible displacement narrative may contain plotlines of escape from injustices which are highly sensationalized and recognizable, like mass rape (Hesford, *Spectacular*). While much of the scholarship I employ in this chapter focuses on the narratives of refugees, I use these works to frame my argument that both people seeking refuge and asylum are mandated to provide credible narratives of their (fear of) persecution, albeit in different processes.

The narrative standards described here demonstrate an ideology that storytelling is centered on persuasion and dominance; ironically, the listener (the U.S. asylum system) holds the power and can empower the "asylum-seeker"/storyteller, so long as they relay hegemonic victimization narratives based on Western literary tropes. The empowerment that an "asylum-seeker" receives through the nation-state (opportunities to work, reunite with families, or remain in the U.S.) simultaneously disempowers them as they endure the label of victim. Suffice it to say, the underlying common theme of credible displacement narratives is the perpetuation of Western power throughout the postcolonial world (Hesford; Powell). In fact, Powell posits that Western involvement in displacement narratives is "to know that we [western audiences] are not them [displaced]" (*Identity* 189). These obstacles made me consider how LPP, as a distinct site within the rhetorical ecology of the U.S. asylum system, supports clients in navigating such "intersections between public policy narratives and personal narratives" (Shuman and Bohmer 395) in order to help clients become more effective storytellers within the rhetorical ecology.

Defining and Recognizing Echoes of Displacement

Echoes of displacement is a term inspired by Powell's *Identity and Power in Narratives of Displacement*, in which she describes how understanding "multiple layers of displacement" or "the ways that identity, narrative, public policy, and legislation intersect and interact" (189) is a pivotal starting point when reading asylum narratives observations on this issue. In other words, when listening to narratives from people seeking asylum, it is paramount to engage with the associated and multilayered transnational and neocolonial contexts in order to become "cognizant of the wider vectors of power that impact these individual [people's] lived experiences" (Dingo, "Macro and Micro," 539), especially focusing on how rhetorics shift and transform across situated sites and borders to the peril or benefit of the individual. Because people seeking asylum are usually required to share these public narratives shortly after arriving in the U.S., their narrative reactions are fresh resonances—echoes—of the lived experiences that people may have endured prior to seeking asylum. In order to capture such reverberations, those who hear asylum narratives must exercise "rhetorical listening" (Ratcliffe) that requires a meaningful pause—similar to the pause required when listening to an echo—in order to understand and appreciate its significance.

One such echo that needs attention is selective silence, which, as I show below, is a reverberation of the silence that clients have previously enacted as a response to their persecution within their previous rhetorical ecologies. In other words, their silence is an echo of the silence they are already used to performing in order to survive and escape within their country of origin; thus, when carefully listened to (Foss and Griffin; Ratcliffe) within the rhetorical network that is LPP, these silences are meaningful and revealing about the nuances of clients' (fear of) persecution.

To help me understand silence as an echo of displacement, and consequently silence and listening as marked shelter rhetorics, I align with feminist rhetorics and social science scholarship within displacement contexts. In feminist rhetorical studies, selective silence has been observed "as a rhetoric, whether it's used for domination, persuasion, or, best of all, rhetorical listening that leads to understanding" (Glenn 283). Feminist rhetoricians Cheryl

Glenn and Krista Ratcliffe have explored the ways in which the arts of silence and listening "have been conceptualized and employed in different times and places by many different people—some with power, some without—for purposes as diverse as showing reverence, gathering knowledge, planning action, buying time, and attempting to survive" (2). One of the key arguments that Glenn and Ratcliffe make is that "the arts of silence and listening offer people multiple ways to negotiate and deliberate, whether with themselves or in dyadic, small-group, or large-scale situations" (3). In this chapter, I rely on the concept of "rhetorical listening," or how listening is a strategy of rhetorical invention, like reading, writing, and speaking, that leads to "cross-cultural dialogues" of understanding (Ratcliffe 196). I also lean on the concept of invitational rhetoric that promotes listening in order to "create an environment that facilitates understanding, accords value and respect to others' perspectives, and contributes to the development of relationships of equality" (Foss and Griffin 17). Invitational rhetoric's chief purpose is to understand rather than persuade.

These key ideas about the underlying rhetorical value of silence and listening coincide with work done within displacement contexts from the social sciences which ideologize silence as a strategy for displaced people to tell stories on their own terms and at their own pace (De Haene et al.; McFadyen; Puvimanasinghe et al.). I observed how clients who described that they were not accustomed to talking about their oppression in their native countries often experienced challenges when having to reveal stories of persecution within the U.S. asylum context. The demand for narrative proof within the U.S. asylum context, however, often overshadows these echoes, and the danger is that these narratives, which exhibit silences, are deemed inauthentic.

"We Learn to Endure Everything Ourselves": Selective Silence

People seeking asylum may be already accustomed to using silence as a rhetorical strategy to help them resist the cultural shame that accompanies various kinds of persecution, rape being one obvious example. Issa was one client who participated in this study who shared about how her rape, which was used as a means of political oppression, was culturally and legally erased. She attributes her silence to the local narrative norms within her community: "I am from deep rural areas. Things like this, you don't even talk about them. Like, a woman who has been raped—people will think you went out looking for it." For Issa, the consequences of revealing her rape to her local community are costly and layered, especially in how her story culturally identifies her as sexually immoral. In her effort to shape her identity with the story, Issa remained silent while in her country. This choice contrasts with Issa's decision to reveal this tragic experience to an asylum officer in the U.S. in order to obtain refuge. Issa explains: "Some things have been kept in the family, even if it is eating you up, it's just, we're raised in a different way. No matter how hard it is, you just have to keep bottling things up. Yeah, so, coming to this side, being asked or talking about [rape] was very difficult, and you have no choice but to say it."

Issa interprets both of her rhetorical ecologies (native community and U.S. asylum context) as contexts in which she has no narrative choice. From a rhetorical standpoint, however, Issa is experiencing how her networked rhetorical location in which she finds herself is able to powerfully constrain how she tells her story in order to save her life (physical, social, cultural). Issa's rape, which is a highly recognizable form of oppression in the Global North (Hesford, *Spectacular*), now allows her to be easily categorized as a "victim" within human rights narrative frameworks (Matua 1). This is because Issa's rhetorical identity (re)formation (Reynolds, "Location")—from sexually immoral woman to victim—is contingent on her ecology and opens up the opportunity to access necessary support like health services and the right to apply for asylum, which can lead to a life within a safe(r) country. Social science work within refugee contexts concurs that people who are displaced may use silence to help them reshape "a narrative identity that [is] more acceptable" within their rhetorical contexts (Puvimanasinghe et al. 88). So, Issa's decision to ultimately share her story of persecution may allow her to win her asylum case because her rape narrative plays into the archetypal refugee experience and identity, and through "drawing on these 'familiar' plots, an applicant bolsters the plausibility and persuasiveness of [their] own tale" (Holland 89). In other words, Issa experiences a crucially significant and fast-paced shift in rhetorical ecology which, at the very least, demonstrates how silence manifests as an echo of the oppression some have experienced at the intersection of story, culture, and persecution.

What is more, rhetorical silence may correlate with someone's inexperience with the narrative demand for details and specificity, integral parts of establishing credibility through narrative in the U.S. asylum process (Holland). Revealing details of such intimately tragic experiences may not be expected or welcomed outside of U.S. culture. For example, Issa eventually told her mother about her rape, but withheld any details from her because in "African culture you don't talk to your mom in such a way." This shows how the credible fear interview and the U.S. asylum application itself operate as a "cultural performance in which applicants, … officials, lawyers, and others who assist in the process … renegotiate identities and reconfigure differing conceptions of trauma, of suffering, and, especially, of what asylum means" (Shuman and Bohmer 410). But if people seeking asylum are not savvy about how to establish a culturally approved ethos within their new ecologies (as in providing ample detail), the U.S. asylum system may read their silences and omissions as an indication of deceit. The silences may, in fact, be an echo of the sociopolitical norms of storytelling that work to silence victims, like women who have been raped.

Other clients I spoke to seemed to use silence as an echo of their previous communities' corruption. When I asked Ayana if she reported her persecution to authorities in her native country, she explained, "you say to yourself, 'why am I going to go to the police?' That is, 'why am I going to tell my story to someone that isn't going to help me?'" In other words, silence may be a reaction or reverberation to the ongoing, systematic absence of support to which someone seeking asylum has already been adapted, so speaking about these experiences to government authorities may be unfamiliar, stressful, and seem futile. Ayana's silence demonstrates, in a material way, Cooper's rhetorical observation of how each rhetor and message are circumscribed by the other rhetors and messages within the contextualized network (372). Accordingly, the corruption that permeates such contextualized rhetorical networks can silence death and the cause of death for some, as was the case for Issa's partner. Issa explained that her native government falsified her partner's death certificate to erase the political persecution of his torture that ultimately killed him. The official document, which may have been proof of Issa's claim for asylum, continues to silence her family's tragedy and is still powerfully missing from her own claim.

Still another cause for selective silence may stem from the normalization of retaliation on those who report injustices within their native country. Indeed, Kourtney, a social work student who interned at the shelter, also insightfully noted how after arriving in a safe country, those seeking refuge "may have come to terms with their reality and may have normalized the danger they were experiencing before they left their country." Perhaps Alex's story is what taught me most about this. His body bore the traces of persecution from his country of origin; his burn scars, which he revealed to me and are only visible on his feet, are the traces left by the police from his country of origin which he claims targeted him partly because of his skin color and ethnic background. I was surprised when he admitted that he did not originally share his scars during his credible fear interview. He was troubled by the amount of information he had to share during this process in order to establish his case because his experiences in his country of origin had conditioned him and his community to "learn to endure everything ourselves," without telling others.

As Alex laughed nervously in disbelief at what he described as an "American" demand for such proof, he explained how someone from his country would not discuss or reveal such markings because of fear, shame, and a propensity toward secrecy as a citizen of his authoritative government. Issa, like Alex, understands the complex connection between selective silence and safety. Indeed, scholars who study asylum narratives have observed the layered agency within silence in that "elected mutism" may be a form of control and survival that protects individuals from the unknown consequences of stories which make them personally vulnerable (McFadyen 9). For example, Issa shared how after her rape, in which she was beaten unconscious, she could not go to the hospital for necessary medical care because of the hospital's connection with the corrupt government. She explained to me, "if you have been beaten, you just keep quiet. You can't just go to a hospital if you are raped, they are not allowed to touch me without a police report if I am raped, so I am incriminating myself if I go to the hospital." Such experiences can even cause deep misunderstandings for people seeking asylum about how "persecution" is defined within their new rhetorical ecology. Kourtney has observed that certain types of oppression can be culturally normalized, such as sexual violence or exploitation of women or children, and some people seeking asylum would not understand that such acts are deemed "persecution" or cause for "fear of persecution" within U.S. contexts; so they may remain silent about certain experiences out of simply misinterpreting the basic conditions of refuge.

Deeply listening to Alex's and Issa's silence about their corporeal proof of persecution helps us notice that their omissions are a meaningful reverberation of the very type of oppression they faced in their native countries which demanded their silence of their respective abuse. Viewing silence this way shows how they work as "sites of knowledge in themselves, providing substance to a story. The stumbling pregnant pauses and gaps in a narrative can refer to unspeakable events" (McFadyen 8). By listening to this echo of displacement (Alex's selective silence about his burn scars or Issa's initial choice to not speak of her rape), not only do we get a sense of how deeply ingrained their reaction to persecution had become, but it also allows us to trace how they have coped with persecution through silence and why their stories, and others like them, may not include such detailed accounts or proofs of credible fear in the first place.

Once Alex's lawyer discovered his scars, Alex was advised to include information about them on his official application. No doubt, Alex was experiencing what many asylum applicants face when working with legal representation: a cultural narrative shift in the kind of stories that "correspond with current Western social values" (Shuman and Bohmer 398), or simply what Alex referred to as "American" narrative demands. Alex's narrative reaction is partly due to Holland's estimation of asylum applicant's assumption that "they may tell [their story] the way they understand it, the way they want to tell it, rather than the way the asylum system requires it." Alex exemplifies just that; people seeking asylum "struggle with understanding what the American bureaucracy wants to hear" because of the abrupt shift within rhetorical ecology that many seeking asylum experience (Holland 90).

In sum, such struggles with selective silence, as a survival strategy, are in direct tension with the rhetorical ecology that is the U.S. asylum system. Those who decide to tell their stories, using the narrative norms that Alex labels "American," experience firsthand the jarring fluidity of a rhetorical ecology. My respondents have become acutely aware that their position as rhetors, their message, and their audience are not stable, but are dependent on a "wider sphere of active, historical, and lived processes" (Edbauer 8).

Because this awareness can be painfully jolting, people seeking asylum require a Third Space, or a space which allows them to slowly and discursively construct their own spaces based on non-binary, often contradictory, messy rhetorics. Third Spaces allow clients to tell stories on their own terms, in their own time, for their own alternative purposes (Flores), and doing so is made possible by an environment which demonstrates a sensitivity to their silence as a rhetorical reverberation, or echo of their displacement.

"Here, It Is Like a Little Hospital": Community Building and Trust

Many clients commented how the shelter offered a peaceful place to stay alongside people who had experienced similar trauma, and this camaraderie is fundamental for allowing clients to build community in order to consider sharing their stories. For example, David remarked that the other clients are his "colleagues" and that he is able to relate to their suffering or at least observe that some have "worse" stories than he does: "Here, it is like a little hospital. You come, you think you are very, very, very sick. Arriving at the hospital, you found maybe there is another one who they cut their limb. Psychologically, I think, 'Okay, David, you are not alone having problems. So many people have problem, and they are now safe. They can live here.'"

David's perception of LPP as a space of shared experiences of varied trauma provides relief, even as an opportunity to compare and gauge his own suffering with that of others. By juxtaposing his experiences of loss with someone who has experienced the loss of a limb, David is renegotiating his story, identity, and chances of recovery and survival, as seen in his hospital analogy. Without verbalizing his story to his "colleagues," David exercises "rhetorical listening" (Ratcliffe) of their varied narratives as well as his own by "standing under" his fellow clients' narratives and "consciously integrating this information into [his] world-views and decision-making" (Ratliffe 206).

In this way, he is impacted by his rhetorical ecology because he locates himself within it, especially the rhetorical possibilities and implications of the variety of stories which he observes. Through adopting an "invitational rhetoric" which leans on understanding instead of persuasion (Foss and Griffin 17), David is able to notice the fluidity of his own perspective as impacted by the storied lives of his community, a hallmark of rhetorical ecology (Edbauer 18). What is more, David's thoughts put a new light on the well-established perspective that an asylum narrative "is always told in the presence of another implying a process of negotiation between the various actors involved" (Burki 5). Instead of focusing on the bureaucratic co-actors involved, David's thoughts remind us that displaced individuals already introspectively listen to their own narratives, comparing their own stories with those displaced lives around them in order to identify commonalities and contrasts that may aid them in survival.

Clients also commented how LPP's home-like atmosphere and community has allowed them to simply focus on their own humanity, safety, and dignity; thus, they are not overwhelmed by the need to tell their story aloud or in writing during their stay. Through focusing on their own human rights, regardless of their asylum narratives, shelter clients invite us to listen to their lived experiences in new ways (Foss and Griffin), especially allowing them to redefine themselves—apart from being an "asylum-seeker"—and their lived experiences—apart from fear and persecution (Zepeda 145).

For example, Benjamin was a client who described how he feels free at LPP, especially the ways the Sisters are like mothers to him with their "beautiful, good love" and "motherly love." He admits that the Sisters correct him because he calls them "mother" as he feels they treat him with a "mother's love." He also laughed playfully when he described the cement pathway leading to Casa Maria which he calls "freedom way" (Figure 4.1). The path leads to the office phone where he can call his loved ones in Africa as well as to the dining room where he chooses his own food for breakfast. This freedom of choice and connection provides a sense of liberty that he did not have in detention where each morning a loud call would signal breakfast and he spent many hours isolated. For Benjamin, LPP is "beautiful," "silent," and markedly different from his experience in immigration detention facilities where he endured high levels of anxiety as well as symptoms of depression, such as self-harm.

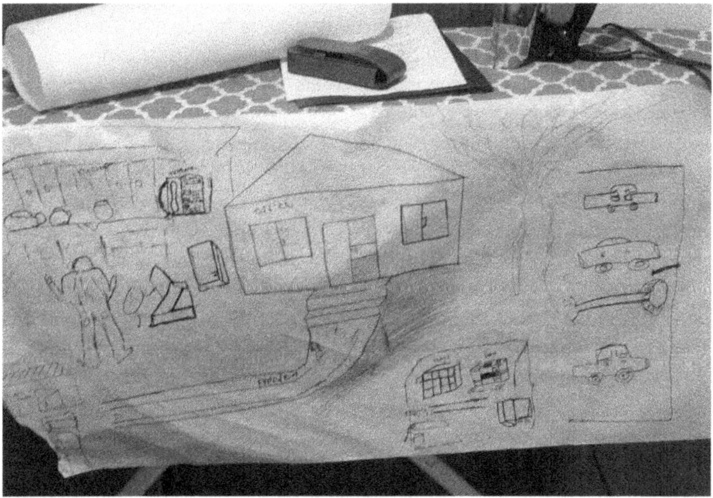

Figure 4.1 "*La Hostería*" shows several material items at LPP that Benjamin found supportive, such as phones, green spaces, a shared bedroom, as well as the kitchen and dining room. Drawing by Benjamin.

In the spirit of creating a Third Space, Benjamin is redefining himself (Zepeda 142) when he chooses to focus on how the shelter nourishes his own humanity and need for family, seen in his insistence to refer to the Sisters as mothers. Benjamin described that while in detention, he was apprehensive about sharing his story of persecution, even during the mandated counseling sessions. He revealed that he didn't trust anyone and felt the need to protect himself from the possibility that his narrative may lead to deportation and further criminalization, two labels that made Benjamin feel shame.

When asked about the shelter's support in helping him create his story, Benjamin perceived the staff and materials as reinforcing his own self-identification and autonomy because at the shelter he is not an inmate or "asylum-seeker"; he is simply a human being who is lovable and worthy of respect.

Yazmin is another client with a similar perspective. She claimed that there is no support at the shelter to help her prepare for telling her story within the asylum process. Instead, like Benjamin, she focused on LPP as a space for rest, safety, meals, and companionship, aligning with staff member Leticia's perspective of LPP as a "simple, little shelter." Yazmin initially revealed that, from her vantage point, the staff help clients with travel arrangements, but they don't necessarily help clients with the legal process of asylum, like composing narratives for an application. While Yazmin did later remember that she met volunteer lawyers who visited LPP and that clients were able to talk and ask for advice on their cases through a free consultation with these volunteer lawyers, she could not remember what their advice was.

Among other things, Yazmin's forgettable experience with the volunteer lawyers demonstrates the compartmentalization of her own role in her family's asylum process. She describes how when her family was preparing to make the trip to the U.S., she imagined that they would have to share their testimony about why they left their country of origin, but it was her husband who carried the burden of preparing to share police documents as well as bodily proof from his bullet wounds. Additionally, while the thought of having to share such traumatic details made her nervous, she didn't expect to be the one to share them because she relied on her husband to speak for the family group. Certainly, Yazmin's spotlight on the shelter as an emotionally supportive community as opposed to a site of legal support in helping her compose her application relates to her role as a new mother whose primary focus was to reunite with her husband and find a home for their growing family.

Yazmin gave birth at the shelter during her three-month stay. She admits how alone she felt after being separated from her husband in detention, indicating the importance of emotional support that LPP provides:

> From the moment we were separated, I didn't feel well because, since I was pregnant, I was more sensitive, so I felt very alone. I didn't know where to go. Since I didn't have anywhere to go, I got very sick. I was depressed for some time, and I didn't know where I would go, where I would give birth to my daughter and all that stuff, and when I would be

able to see [my husband] again because, at the time, we couldn't even talk on the cell phone. I didn't know where he was. I didn't know anything about him, so I felt very bad, and well, things started getting better once I arrived [at LPP] and I had a roof over my head, where to sleep, and things started getting better with time because I was able to talk to him. I knew where he was.

(Yazmin)

Indeed, Yazmin's initial thoughts about LPP as a place of refuge and not necessarily a guide in the asylum process indicate her own ability to self-define as first a human and then as a committed partner and mother. She, like Benjamin, is primarily focused on her human rights—safety, physical and mental health, and shelter for herself and her daughter. This shows that by focusing on their basic needs, instead of their needs as "asylum-seekers" who must compose a persuasive argument within the U.S. asylum system, Yazmin and Benjamin both shift our rhetorical intent when we listen to them. They both call us to an "invitational rhetoric" (Foss and Griffin) in that they are not intending to persuade us (as in classical rhetoric) with stories of their credible fear; instead, they self-define as humans first when they rhetorically offer their perspectives and shift the asylum conversation to focus on their humanity. In fact, Foss and Griffin argue that "invitational rhetoric," which both Benjamin and Yazmin exercise here, is grounded in the foundational idea that rhetors are "the authorities on their own lives" and have "the capacity and right to constitute their worlds as they choose" (4).

I admit that as I first heard Benjamin and Yazmin share about the support at the shelter, I was confused (and at times even frustrated) with what seemed to be (from my dim perspective) their avoidance to use the resources available at the shelter to write their narratives, continue their cases, and hopefully get to a point to live in less precarity. What I came to understand, through their "invitational rhetoric" which invites us "to enter [their] world and to see it as [they] do" (Foss and Griffin 5), is that they were continuing to compose their stories, but they were doing so within LPP as a Third Space, where they establish the discourse which defines them.

"I Did Not Want to Talk about It": Claiming Time and Agency

Clients at LPP are under no obligation to begin their official asylum application, so there is no expectation for them to share their story of persecution with anyone at the shelter unless they want to. For some like Ayana, this opportunity to not talk about her trauma was a welcomed respite and allowed her time to tell her story on her own terms.

Yes, at first, when I got here, I tried to stay away from people because here, in general, when people get here, [other clients ask] "and how did you

> cross? And what has immigration done to you?" So I would stay away. It's gotten better, but when I first got here, I didn't like to talk … and I didn't want to talk about it. It's normal. It's people's curiosity and more so when they saw my bruises and they would tell me, "What happened to you?" There's even a family here who would tell me, "What must have happened to her? Why did she cross by herself? Is she a little crazy?" [laughs] That's why I would stay away because I didn't like it when people would ask me things. And I did that a lot—just distanced myself because I did not want to talk about it.
>
> (Ayana)

While Ayana's choice to not share her story, even with those who asked, may seem avoidant, her choice is a claim for time to process her trauma and traverse her own unique experiences with persecution and pain (De Haene et al. 1671). Her silences are not an absence of the story; instead, they are substantially part of her story, revealing that she has trauma that is not ready to be told. In Ayana's case, these silences are connected to crossing the border clandestinely into the U.S. and being raped soon after while hiding in the wilderness near the Rio Grande River. Thus, her silences are essentially a "strong way to speak" about her journey and trauma (De Haene et al. 1671), indicated by her resistance to answering the shelter community's questions about her entrance into the country as well as her bruises. In this way, Ayana's choice to be silent demonstrates her unique form of "resilience, empowerment, and agency" about how her story is revealed (McFadyen 10). In fact, Ayana's silence may even be labeled "strategic" because her silence is "purposeful" in that it "resonates with meaning and intention, just like that of the spoken word" (Glenn 282).

Although she didn't speak about her own past to other clients, Ayana did listen to others' stories at LPP, and this culminated within a feminist material space of speaking, listening, and silence (Foss and Griffin; Glenn; Ratcliffe). Ayana was able to capture a photo of the outdoor circular table, "La mesa redonda" (Figure 4.2), to depict the space where she slowly built community with other women every day:

> In the evenings, after dinner, we have free time, some girls would gather there, and sometimes, I would join them. Little by little, I would join them, and all of them would start telling their story, what they used to do in their country or why they came here and things like that. I would listen. I wouldn't share my stuff, but I would listen. I liked to listen. It distracted me, listening to it, each one's story, and it was always like that. We'd start—maybe, we didn't always talk about [the past] but also about our future and all that, so that was something really beautiful that we would do in the evenings, after dinner, there, at the table.
>
> (Ayana)

Figure 4.2 "*La Mesa Redonda*"/"The Round Table" captures a white circular round table with connected benches outside Casa Belen under a large tree. Photo by Ayana.

Ayana's initial hesitance to tell her story but willingness to listen to others' stories demonstrates how LPP offers a foil to the accelerated, persuasive-driven demand for credibility narratives within the U.S. asylum system that centers on criminalizing people who seek asylum.

First, the rhetorical intents of sharing a story of persecution are different at the outdoor round table than during a credible fear interview; the former is based on "rhetorical listening" (Ratcliffe) and "invitational rhetoric" (Foss and Griffin), while the latter is based on classical rhetorical perspectives of persuasion. Ayana and the women she joined at the table are thus fulfilling their need for "adequate space to tell their stories at their own pace and in a manner most conducive to them" (Puvimanasinghe et al. 70). This self-paced rhetorical exchange/listening is especially seen in Ayana's description of how she became part of the group "little by little." In this way, the outdoor circular table is a critical networking site at LPP for those seeking asylum, especially women, in that it offers habitual meeting space for those who voluntarily desire to listen and speak among other displaced women without the same bureaucratic high-stakes like those in an asylum hearing.

Second, the community and storytelling that takes place here is in stark contrast to the storytelling that demarcates lines of difference between mainstream or bureaucratic audiences in the Global North and those who seek asylum. Instead, the outdoor round table allows Ayana to experience stories as "empowering for refugee and immigrant women" because they are "told among friends" and "told in a language or talk style that is comfortable to them," and this provides Ayana and the other women "space to voice themselves" (Hua 113). As a rhetor, Ayana has slowly been able to gauge the rhetorical possibilities at this table and make meaning at her own pace and in collaboration with women who may have faced similar circumstances. *La mesa redonda* is a space for Ayana and the other women to practice what Cheryl Glenn refers to as the "feminist rhetorical art" of silence which works to "resist" powerful bureaucracies that would use the words of marginalized people to reduce and categorize them (262). This practice is characteristic of a Third Space because it is a daily activity the community sees as significant in self-defining and re-visioning their lived experiences (Flores 145). This is especially seen in Ayana's description of storytelling about the past and future as "beautiful" because there is a beauty in simply letting such stories be offered, shared, and heard without the need to persuade an audience (Foss and Griffin; Ratcliffe).

Still, sharing stories, even stories of hope or inspiration, is sometimes problematic for staff and volunteers; in fact, most I interviewed were apprehensive when I asked them to share an example of a "success story" about a client who inspired them or may inspire others (clients or mainstream audiences). Mary, an LPP volunteer of many years, was eventually able to share one brief example of a young man who confided in her; she sums up his experience as successful simply in that "he had trusted me in talking about [his persecution]." On the other hand, Timotheo completely resisted sharing a "success story" that he would share with clients. Such stories, for him, are troubling in that client narratives can offset emotional trauma in others: "When I was here before [as a client], I would hear other people's stories, and I would get more sadder. My advice is: don't listen to others. Each case is different."

Both Mary and Timotheo's reluctance to share a representative story of success within the asylum context is telling in that they refuse to provide a narrative that abstracts or epitomizes the asylum experience. Timotheo's reaction uniquely shows he has developed a transnational rhetorical perspective of his responsibility within this rhetorical ecology, namely, that stories should be contextualized in order to showcase the nuances and differences in displacement experience. Along similar lines, Mary is decidedly quiet about her volunteer work with friends and family: "I don't tell even people at home. I just tell that what they hear on the radio is not, not too good or too right." When people ask her if what the news depicts is accurate, she tells them that the images are true about the "many, many people" that cross through the Texas border and describes the state of immigration simply as a "shame." While Mary does not explain her choice to stay silent about her volunteer work within her native community, she implies later in our interview how confidentiality is of utmost importance to her as a mark of trust in her relationship with clients.

Both Mary and Timotheo, then, use silence as a way to shelter clients from emotional trauma or scrutiny, and most importantly, neither desire the power or responsibility that comes from listening to or circulating such stories. I argue that this is due to the chaotic and divisive asylum issue within their rhetorical ecology of the U.S. including the southern Texas border (Chapter 3). Mary and Timotheo's responses show that they have organically learned that if an "asylum success story" is to be valued, appreciated, and understood, "it involves not only the offering of the rhetor's perspective but the creation of an atmosphere [that is grounded in] safety, value, and freedom" (Foss and Griffin 10). Within the invitational rhetoric framework that Foss and Griffin propose, safety implies that rhetors are secure from "danger" (10); value implies that rhetors will treat one another as autonomous equals, especially avoiding condescending responses which "attempt to fit [rhetors] into [reductive] roles" (11); and freedom includes the liberty to express perspectives "without the possibility of losing the respect of the rhetor" (13).

Mary and Timotheo's reactions imply that safety is missing on a variety of levels for clients within this rhetorical ecology, especially in that their stories are key for refuge in material ways. In fact, Timotheo shares how he warns clients not to share stories with one another: "sometimes I tell them not to talk about it with, with each other. The advice I give them—don't talk about your situation because sometimes there are people who have a different problem and another person might laugh and make you feel uncomfortable." Timotheo saw personal stories as vulnerabilities which may be used against others in moments of contention among clients: "Sometimes, we get here, and we're happy, but after living together we might not get along, and we start telling those stories to others, so I tell them, 'Don't share your stories.'"

Value is not guaranteed in this rhetorical ecology either, since telling a story about one person may be dangerously misrepresentative. For example, when Mary does mention to others her volunteerism, her rhetorical emphasis is on the "many" people seeking asylum, thus strategically abstracting the individual in her effort to safeguard the individual narratives and people she serves. Timotheo, on the other hand, emphasizes how "each" individual's experience is different and cannot be summed up in any tidy way or represented in any one story. Both Mary and Timotheo have organically learned, through their years working with displaced people (and Timotheo's own displacement), how storytelling may further harm a person seeking asylum because sharing one story may risk "naturalizing the experiences" through "positivist appeals to experiences and the homogenizing notions of identity" (Hua 112). On the other hand, sharing a plurality of stories at the outdoor round table, as in Ayana's case, is a decolonial and feminist space for rhetorical exchange stemming from clients themselves.

Foss and Griffin's concept of rhetorical freedom is elusive in this rhetorical ecology as well because of the judgment that often accompanies asylum narratives, both morally and legally. Mary explains how she tries "not to question [clients] about how they got here" or ask clients in-depth questions because it is not her intention to know the details of their lives: "I don't want them to feel that I'm here to find out about them. If they want to tell me, I'll listen, but I don't want to be nubby. And I've seen many visitors come, and all they do is ask questions, 'why? why? why?' And I never ask why? [LPP] is here to help them, to help them start off in this country, and I don't want them to think I'm, I'm just nubby."

By consciously not probing for or circulating their stories, Mary is uniquely using silence to respect clients, without having to hear their stories to judge their value or need from the U.S. asylum system. In fact, Mary shares that some people from her hometown are "bitter" about people who seek asylum, and they question, "Why are they coming here?" thus indicating their intent to judge the validity of someone's choice to seek asylum. The selective silence that the clients and staff practice at LPP is part of their agentive practice within their Third Space in that it offers them opportunities for choice which eluded David (mentioned at the chapter's opening) who was open about his desire to keep his story private unless it would help his family to escape persecution.

Indeed, even if clients select to remain silent, obtaining asylum requires them to write their story as part of their application. While they are not pressured to begin that process at the shelter, those who do initiate this task will often rely on LPP's materials, resources, and experience to help them accomplish this. In the next section, I analyze how staff and volunteers work with silence in order to generate stories that can be shared as public narratives of asylum.

"Write Down Your Story" and "A Fighting Chance"

One interesting "success story" that student-intern Kourtney was willing to share did not contain any details about a client's persecution or socioeconomic mobility within the U.S. upon being granted asylum. In fact, Kourtney's example of inspiration has to do with a client who was able to "put aside" the shame of his abuse and persecution "and share his story." Kourtney had worked with a man who had stayed at LPP but had entered the country clandestinely, so crossing the heavily guarded Department of Homeland Security checkpoint that sits just north of the Rio Grande Valley seemed too risky for him. However, it was the only option he could imagine to reunite with his wife and child. In Kourtney's words, the man "decided to be honest about his situation with [shelter] staff," and he wrote his story. After receiving translation services at the shelter, the staff were able to connect him to a lawyer quickly because his experiences, and the recorded version of those experiences, made it possible to expedite his case. The lawyer was able to use this man's written narrative to develop it further and help him submit the application for asylum. This application itself, without being decided yet, was enough for him to obtain a receipt granting him permission to travel within the U.S. and see his family. Kourtney shares, "I love this story because this client persevered through his situation. It would have been so easy for him to attempt to continue his way illegally to Houston out of desperation. He could have also chosen not to share the reason why he made the journey to the US and might have not received the help he received."

On a very practical level, this example demonstrates how LPP functions as what rhetorician Margaret Syverson would call a "complex system" constituted by "self-organizing, adaptive, and dynamic interactions" within a wider rhetorical ecology made up of material affordances. In her work, *The Wealth of Reality: An Ecology of Composition*, Syverson describes how material affordances that allow rhetors to participate in these complex systems include "environmental structures, such as pens, paper, computers, books, telephones, fax machines, photocopiers, printing presses, and other natural and human-constructed features" (5).

These material and everyday tools allow the rhetors at LPP to engage with "other complex systems operating at various levels of scale, such as families, global economies, publishing systems, theoretical frames, academic disciplines, and language itself" (5). To put this into more perspective, the rhetors at LPP must interact and make meaning (sometimes across various languages) with various people and agencies in order to process their claim/narrative for asylum: U.S. Immigration and Citizenship Services, lawyers, volunteers, healthcare workers, LPP staff; detailed international and U.S. policies and guidelines about immigration law (either in print or online); communications that may be difficult to obtain but may serve as proof of their claim, such as news/media reporting and official government documents from their native countries; and communicative tools, such as computers (Figure 4.3), cell phones, email, and traditional mail services.

While looking at LPP as a rhetorical network from such a wide angle can be overwhelming, LPP's approach to supporting clients writing public narratives of asylum shows that they begin by focusing on one local site—the individual themselves. For example, part of Leticia's everyday job at LPP includes encouraging clients to write their narratives down in any language that they feel most comfortable with. She then, with the client's consent, aims to have their narratives translated by French or Spanish-speaking volunteers if necessary. Such a practice, for Leticia, is necessary for success in the U.S. asylum process: "[I tell them to] write your story. Write everything that happened to you. The date. The time. If possible, where, and write your story— What I'm trying to do to help them is to give them like a fighting chance." Leticia's call for clients to "write everything" is her encouragement for clients to transition from silence to writing, describing and detailing their persecution

Figure 4.3 "*La Computadora*"/"The Computer" shows a desktop computer on a desk in the ELL classroom surrounded by the American flag and an angel decoration. Photo by Ayana.

without yet considering how their localized experiences of persecution connect with "a wider sphere of active, historical, and lived processes" such as the U.S. asylum system, a wide rhetorical ecology (Edbauer 8).

However, as shown within this chapter, silence is not readily forsaken. According to Leticia and Kourtney, what often occurs is that clients use this writing exercise to share excerpts of their stories because clients are often accustomed to operating within a rhetorical ecology where silence is used for survival. In fact, within the same example that Kourtney shared, she describes how the initial draft that the client wrote demonstrated "that there were many details he was omitting." This is when shelter staff, like Kourtney and Leticia, seize opportunities to listen to clients' echoes of displacement, like silence, in order to transition them into the rhetorical ecology of the U.S. asylum system by asking questions and making suggestions.

As noted previously, despite the fact that the burden of proof is solely on the applicant to validate their narrative, an asylum narrative is essentially a collaborative product, shared among multiple players within the institutional setting of governmental review, such as the asylum applicant, immigration boards, translators, lawyers, and judges (Burki; Hesford; Mayo; Powell; Vogl; Kjelsvik; Smith-Khan). For example, Vogl and Kjelsvik, respectively, emphasize the various sanctioned agencies and systems (such as U.S. immigration officers and "Credible Fear Interview" guidelines) which rhetorically craft regulations and guidance for processing displaced people, including how to listen and speak to refugees and people seeking asylum in contexts which decide their futures. For shelter staff, the best support that can help clients prepare for how their stories will be heard and perceived by the U.S. government are lawyers. Leticia describes,

> A lawyer should be helping them with the asylum process, but it usually costs about 2,500 to 5,000 dollars, and usually these people don't have that type of money. It's always better, I say, your chances of winning your case increase double or triple fold if you get a lawyer. If you have [your narrative] ready, when you go to the lawyer—you know, they're the lawyer, so they're going to be the ones to develop the story or ask questions, so we get them to the point where they have a fighting chance.
>
> (Leticia)

Kourtney affirms this perspective based on her many years of experience, "experienced attorneys know how to rephrase information in a particular manner for the benefit of the client. A client's case can be negatively affected if inaccurate information is provided." Leticia and Kourtney were acutely aware that the clients' narratives would be scrutinized within the U.S. asylum system, so their writing support was an effort to help clients craft a situated ethos (Kohl and Farthing). Feminist rhetorician Nedra A. Reynolds suggests the "potential of ethos to open up more spaces in which to study writers' subject positions or identity formations, especially to examine how writers establish authority and enact responsibility from positions not traditionally considered authoritative" in shifting "time," "texts," and "spaces" (326). Reynolds' argument is that marginalized rhetors, such as those applying for asylum, are aware of their need to establish ethos (as in "credible fear") in locations without "harmonious communities," or settings that have little to no tidy consensus, shared perspectives, values, and beliefs (329). Reynolds sees the benefits of "emphasizing where and how texts and their writers are located—their intersections with others and the places they diverge, how they occupy positions and move in the betweens" (333). By listening to their echoes, LPP staff are then able to help clients compose their way into the rhetorical ecology by helping them locate themselves within it.

What is more, this assemblage of writing support at LPP demonstrates the "distributive agency" of the public narrative of the asylum experience (Bennett 31). In other words, when viewing the writing support that LPP offers from a rhetorical ecology perspective, it becomes clear that there is no independent agent, or even a hierarchical relationship between agents in the ecology (Bennett 22); instead, each actor in the ecology comprises the rhetorical "mosaic" that is the public narrative that is ultimately shared for legal status (Bennett 21).

Conclusion

This chapter has presented how silence works as an echo of displacement, or the narratives and silences which reflect traces of or reverberated responses to the trauma of persecution and dislocations of home. From a rhetorical standpoint, the concept of echoes of displacement syncs with what Jim W. Corder has argued about how humans "are always seeing, hearing, thinking, living, and saying the [stories] that we and our times make possible and tolerable, a [story] that is the history we can assent to at a given time" (17). I have also shown how building community, respecting silence, and offering writing support are effective ways for LPP to listen deeply to this shelter rhetoric of silence. I have made theoretical connections between such listening and the "rhetorical listening" (Ratcliffe) advocated by feminist rhetoricians, like Cheryl Glenn or Sonja K. Foss and Cindy L. Griffin who propose a shift or alternative in order to achieve mutual understanding grounded in "equality, immanent value, and self-determination" or one's right to name themselves (Foss and Griffin 4). Such a shift requires that we listen to stories of people seeking asylum, including their storied silence, in the context of understanding instead of the context of persuasion (as is the ideological underpinning of storytelling in the U.S. asylum system), especially concerning their right to make a claim to asylum protection (Foss and Griffin; Ratcliffe). I have analyzed how such listening is part of the discursive formation of a Third Space, especially in that silence affords people seeking asylum an opportunity to transcend hegemonic and binary labels about themselves. Despite the efforts of LPP to listen for mutual understanding to such echoes like silence, I do offer some critiques that are significant to consider.

First, I am aware that LPP has the luxury of revisioning the "interactional goal of rhetoric, which has traditionally been one of persuasion to one of understanding" (Glenn 284) with their clients. In other words, the shelter is a unique community and in no way represents how people seeking asylum are being heard and interpreted on a larger scale. LPP, as a small emergency shelter designed to support the individual, allows the community time and space to listen to clients' echoes of displacement in ways that help clients enact agency, often through silence. As Glenn argues, "rhetors using silence will not be participating in the traditional rhetorical discipline of combat and dominance; they will be sharing perceptions, understandings, and power. They will use silence to embody new ways to challenge and resist domination" (Glenn 284). In contrast, the ongoing U.S. policy changes (discussed in Chapter 3) demonstrate how echoes, such as silences, are disregarded in most other contexts where people seeking asylum exist. In fact, some of the changes, like Migrant Protection Protocols ("Remain in Mexico"), only exacerbate the inhibitions that people seeking asylum experience. For example, Remain in Mexico's policies affect the legal access and safety of someone seeking asylum in ways which have recently led to many choosing to return to their countries of origin to escape violence and exploitation in Mexico and/or a decrease in those who are able to attend their court hearings in the U.S. (Foster-Frau).

Secondly, while the shelter offers LPP spaces to exercise silence (as/and) storytelling on their own terms, it also supports clients who desire to tell their stories within a highly problematic, bureaucratic, and reductive rhetorical ecology that is the U.S. asylum system. In other words, the question must be asked: by helping clients write "compelling" public narratives of asylum for their applications (by hegemonic U.S. asylum standards), is LPP only perpetuating the binary-based, inflexible narrative standards of asylum experience that are so difficult to navigate? The complicated answer begins to emerge when we observe how LPP nurtures clients first as human beings to tell stories which fracture the "false sense of stasis" about identity; the community encourages clients to offer stories which highlight the "in-motion and in-process qualities of the displacement where 'moving identities' are constantly in action" (Powell, *Identity* 15). Powell argues that the act of being displaced impacts identity in profound ways, even in the opportunity for a displaced individual to "resist having a narrative identity imposed on them, and create subversive narrative identities as resistance to the subjectivities inscribed on them" (*Identity* 13). In similar ways, and as I've shown in the previous chapter, Chicana feminist Lisa Flores focuses on how those who dwell in border spaces, such as the RGV where LPP is located, are able to discursively create a Third Space through their own storytelling and self-defining. For those who live in such in-betweens, there is often a "fight for space of their own," and the right to name themselves (Flores 143) as a response to hegemonic and essentialist misrepresentations of themselves within mainstream narratives. In other words, LPP offers clients the freedom to tell their stories in ways that they desire, whether that be to persuade U.S. asylum officers or simply to offer their silences and listen to others at a simple outdoor round table—a sliver of the wider Third Space that is LPP.

In the next chapter, I continue my focus on how the daily practices of LPP perpetuate a Third Space, as I did here; however, I offer an analysis of the new stories which clients tell based on their new normal as clients of an in-between shelter. Such new stories allow clients to "explore the moments of resistance, even if subtle, where being 'displaced' is only a part of one's identity" (Powell, *Identity*, 173).

References

Bennett, Jane. *Vibrant Matter: A Political Ecology of Things*. Duke University Press, 2010.

Burki, Marie-Florence. "Exploration into an Asylum-Seeker's Narrative Retelling." Master's Thesis, Université de Neuchâtel, 2013.

Cooper, Marilyn M. "The Ecology of Writing." *College English*, vol. 48, no. 4, 1986, pp. 364–75.

Corder, Jim W. “Argument as Emergence, Rhetoric as Love.” *Rhetoric Review*, vol. 4, no. 1, 1985, pp. 16–32. *Taylor & Francis*, http://www.jstor.org/stable/465760.

De Haene, Lucia, et al. “Holding Harm: Narrative Methods in Mental Health Research on Refugee Trauma.” *Qualitative Health Research*, vol. 20, no. 12, 2010, pp. 1664–76.

Dingo, Rebecca. “Networking the Macro and Micro: Toward Transnational Literacy Practices.” *JAC*, vol. 33, no. 3/4, 2013, pp. 529–52.

Dobrin, Sidney I. “Writing Takes Place.” *Ecocomposition: Theoretical and Pedagogical Approaches*, edited by Christian R. Weisser and Sidney I. Dobrin, State University of New York Press, 2001. pp. 11–25.

Edbauer, Jenny. “Unframing Models of Public Distribution: From Rhetorical Situation to Rhetorical Ecologies.” *Rhetoric Society Quarterly*, vol. 35, no. 4, 2005, pp. 5–24.

Flores, Lisa A. “Creating Discursive Space through a Rhetoric of Difference: Chicana Feminists Craft a Homeland.” *Quarterly Journal of Speech*, vol. 82, no. 2, 1996, pp. 142–56, *Routledge*.

Foss Sonja K. and Cindy L. Griffin. “Beyond Persuasion: A Proposal for an Invitational Rhetoric.” *Communication Monographs*, vol. 62, 1995, pp. 2–18, *EBSCO*.

Foster-Frau, Silvia. “Obstacles Mount for Remain in Mexico Migrants.” *San Antonio Express*, 20 Sep. 2020, https://www.expressnews.com/news/local/article/Obstacles-mount-for-Remain-in-Mexico-15570211.php.

Glenn, Cheryl. “A Rhetorical Art for Resisting Discipline(s).” *JAC*, vol. 22, no. 2, 2002, pp. 261–91. https://www.jstor.org/stable/20866487.

Hesford, Wendy S. *Spectacular Rhetorics*. Duke UP, 2011.

Holland, Madeline. “Stories for Asylum: Narrative and Credibility in the United States’ Political Asylum Application.” *Refuge*, vol. 34, no. 2, 2018, pp. 85–93.

Hua, Anh. “Travel and Displacement: An (Ex)Refugee and (Ex)Immigrant Woman’s Tale-Tell.” *Canadian Woman’s Studies*, vol. 19, no. 4, 2000, pp. 110–14.

Kjelsvik, Bjørghild. “‘Winning a Battle, But Losing the War’: Contested Identities, Narratives, and Interaction in Asylum Interviews.” *Text & Talk*, vol. 34, no. 1, 2014, pp. 89–115. *JSOTR*, doi: 10.1515/text-2013-0039.

Kohl, Benjamin and Linda C. Farthing. “Navigating Narrative: The Antinomies of ‘Mediated’ Testimonios.” *The Journal of Latin American and Caribbean Anthropology*, vol. 18, no. 1, 2004, pp. 90–107. *EBSCO*, doi: 10.1111/jlca.12004.

Mayo, Jessica. “Court-Mandated Story Time: The Victim Narrative in U.S. Asylum Law.” *Washington University Law Review*, vol. 89, no. 6, 2012, pp. 1485–1522. *EBSCO*, http://openscholarship.wustl.edu/law_lawreview/vol89/iss6/10.

McFadyen, Gillian. “Memory, Language and Silence: Barriers to Refuge within the British Asylum System.” *Journal of Immigrant & Refugee Studies*, 2018, pp. 1–17. *Sage*, doi: 10.1080/15562948.2018.1429697.

Mutua, Makau. “Savages, Victims, and Saviors: The Metaphor of Human Rights.” *Harvard International Law Journal*, vol. 42, no. 1, 2001, pp. 201–45, *EBSCO*.

Powell, Katrina M. *Identity and Power in Narratives of Displacement*. Routledge, 2015.

Puvimanasinghe, Teresa, et al. “Narrative and Silence: How Former Refugees Talk about Loss and Past Trauma.” *Journal of Refugee Studies*, vol. 28, no. 1, 2015, pp. 69–92. *EBSCO*, doi: 10.1093/jrs/feu019.

Ratcliffe, Krista. “Rhetorical Listening: A Trope for Interpretive Invention and a ‘Code of Cross-Cultural Conduct.’” *College Composition and Communication*, vol. 51, no. 2, 1999, pp. 195–224. doi: 10.2307/359039.

Reynolds, Nedra. "Ethos as Location: New Sites for Understanding Discursive Authority." *Rhetoric Review*, vol. 11, no. 2, 1993, pp. 325–38. *JSTOR*, https://www.jstor.org/stable/465805.

Shuman, Amy and Carol Bohmer. "Representing Trauma: Political Asylum Narrative." *Journal of American Folklore* vol. 117, no. 466, 2004, pp. 394–414, https://doi.org/10.1353/jaf.2004.0100.

Smith-Khan, Laura. "Telling stories: Credibility and the Representation of Social Actors in Australian Asylum Appeals." *Discourse & Society*, vol. 28, no. 5, 2017, pp. 512–34. *Sage*, doi: 10.1177/0957926517710989.

Somers, Margaret R. "The Narrative Constitution of Identity: A Relational and Network Approach." *Theory and Society*, vol. 23, no. 5, 1994, pp. 605–49. *ResearchGate*, doi: 10.1007/BF00992905.

Steimel, Sarah J. "Refugees as People: The Portrayal of Refugees in American Human Interest Stories." *Journal of Refugee Studies*, vol. 23, no. 2, 2010, pp. 219–237. *Sage*, doi: 10.1093/jrs/feq019.

Syverson, Margaret. *The Wealth of Reality: An Ecology of Composition*. Southern Illinois UP, 1999.

Vogl, Anthea. "Telling Stories from Start to Finish: Exploring the Demand for Narrative in Refugee Testimony." *Griffith Law Review*, vol. 22, no. 1, 2013, pp. 63–86. *Routledge*, doi: 10.1080/10383441.2013.10854767.

Weaver, Hilary N., et al. "Asylum Seekers along the U.S.-Canada Border: Challenges of a Vulnerable Population." *Journal of Immigrant & Refugee Services*, vol. 1, no. 3/4, 2003, pp. 81–98. doi: 10.1300/J191v01n03_05.

Zepeda, Candace. "Chicana Feminism." *Decolonizing Rhetoric & Composition Studies*, edited by Iris D. Ruiz and Raul Sánchez, Palgrave Macmillan, 2019, pp. 137–51.

5 Cooking, Crocheting, *y Cantando*

Composing Agency through Routine

One afternoon at La Posada Providencia (LPP) as lunch was finishing, a woman from Central America who had been staying at the shelter for about a month informed a young man from Asia that it was his turn to help with washing the dishes after lunch. This young man had only arrived at the shelter a few days prior. He replied quickly and seriously to her comment, by informing her that in his country, men do not help with kitchen chores. At this, the young woman smiled and confidently reminded him, "Well, you are not in your country anymore!" Her retort caused the dining table of clients from other Central American and African countries to erupt with laughs and cheers.

As I interpreted for them using Spanish and English, I wondered how this playful, cross-cultural, bilingual banter about a routine chore at the shelter worked to position clients within a "new normal," a normal that is unique to LPP as a distinct site that rests within the in-betweens and exists as part of the rhetorical ecology of the U.S. asylum system. I was also curious about what this young woman was signifying when she essentially told her counterpart how quickly he must revise and shift his meaning-making because he was now embodied within a new rhetorical network, which is constantly negotiating with other expanding networks within the larger rhetorical ecology where he wages a claim for asylum.

I appreciate this story because it demonstrates how LPP provides clients opportunities to perform revised roles and tell new stories about themselves, based on the routine, daily, and material interactions afforded by the space. This chapter analyzes clients' routine practices at the shelter to help illustrate the kinds of agentive discourses which emerge from quotidian life within LPP, a rhetorical network within the larger rhetorical ecology of the U.S. asylum system. In contrast with the public narratives of asylum that clients often compose within the shelter (Chapter 4), this chapter illustrates the efficacy of the quiet, semi-private yet robust rhetorics of daily life which allow clients to compose a unique Third Space. I argue that routine—a distinct shelter rhetoric—allows clients to assemble stories which demonstrate alternative rhetorics of displacement that culminate in unique opportunities for agency and naming themselves, hallmarks of a Third Space.

DOI: 10.4324/9781003349693-5

In what follows, I first revisit the hegemonic narratives which surround asylum experience in the U.S. to demonstrate that mainstream narratives of asylum experience (such as narratives found in popular news outlets) reinforce an ideology that asylum experience is fixated on helplessness, loss, and victimization which can only be remedied through the nation-state. I then describe scholarship which has explored how alternatives to such discourses are present in displaced people's materiality of their everyday life and routines. With the support of rhetorical ecology's concept of materiality, cultural rhetorics' concept of "there-ness," and Chicana feminism's concept of "rhetoric of difference," I then present client data to discuss how routines, like crocheting, housework, and singing, allow LPP to use their daily activities as a "*rasquache* rhetoric" (Medina-López) to compose new stories about their lived experiences as people seeking asylum. These *rasquache* rhetorics position LPP clients "in the center" in order to "refuse to accept a marginal identity" (Flores 146).

Hegemonic Discourses of Asylum Experience

Before expounding on the alternative stories that clients tell about themselves within LPP, it is important to review the hegemonic discourses about displacement that clients may bear and desire to negotiate or repudiate. Previous scholarship in both rhetoric and refugee studies demonstrates how mainstream stories in the Global North depict people seeking asylum as helpless victims. For example, Peter Gale's work describes how news media is able to represent people seeking asylum as needy and helpless through individual stories of suffering as well as centralizing images of displaced people's faces instead of capturing visualizations of mass groups (327), while Nelson Phillips and Cynthia Hardy analyze how political cartoons keep a complicated balance of representing displaced people as frauds, victims, as well as a problematic version of both (16–17). Steimel's scholarship summarizes the predominant narratives of asylum neatly by arguing that news media human interest stories in the U.S. commonly represent refugees as "(a) as prior victims; (b) as in search of the American Dream; and (c) as unable to achieve the American Dream" (Steimel, "Refugees," 219). The dangers of such depictions, according to Steimel, include the perpetuation of stereotypical and even racist frameworks in which to understand displaced people's persecution as well as their home country or culture ("Refugees," 232). Moreover, hegemonic perspectives of displaced people as victims also stem from media reporting that depicts life in terms of loss and family separation. These victimization narratives also include the assumption that the Global North is the anecdote to their perceived helplessness, complete with neoliberal, capitalist strategies often accompanied by paternalistic control, commonly seen in human rights narratives (Rajaram).

Steimel argues that these predominant stories help shape the everyday lives of displaced people in the U.S. because they color "public discourses on immigration and refugee policy, the development and availability of social programmes for refugees, and to a large extent, the very social climate refugees face in their everyday lives" (Steimel, "Refugees," 220). In light of such narratives, I began to notice how clients' stories about routine life at the shelter—the life afforded to them in that moment—helped them compose alternatives to such reductive portrayals of asylum experience, especially that the nation-state is their exclusive pathway to the agency.

Agency through Normalcy

Previous scholarship in the fields of rhetoric and communication that studies how displaced people compose alternative rhetorics concludes how focusing on the quotidian offers glimpses of the "moments of resistance, even if subtle, where being 'displaced' is only a part of one's identity" (Powell 173). In Katrina M. Powell's *Identity and Power in Narratives of Displacement*, she articulates how "everyday activities ... are exactly the kind of displacement narratives often overlooked" because the predominant narratives of struggle and success are privileged (172). Similarly, Sarah Steimel's "Negotiating Refugee Empowerment(s) in Resettlement Organizations" offers critical insight into the disconnect between perceptions of empowerment between resettlement agencies and their clients. Steimel argues that while resettlement agencies define agency in terms of economic mobility, the refugee clients they worked with "instead constructed empowerment(s) in economic, educational, personal, and family terms," such as the routine act of being able to care for their own children before school each day ("Empowerment(s)" 102). This dissonance results in displaced people experiencing feelings of disempowerment because they are unable to satisfy their own perceptions of the agency or those of the resettlement organization (which are often conflated with U.S. policies and goals) (Steimel, "Empowerment(s)" 103).

As discussed in Chapter 2, I lean on the concept of materiality from rhetorical ecology studies, especially new materialism (Bennett; Gries et al.) and "there-ness," from cultural rhetorics (Riley-Mukavetz). Materiality has to do with the rhetorical agency of relationships between all matter—humans, non-humans, objects, and spaces (Gries et al. 86), while "thereness" "draws attention to the significance of located everyday tasks" in the formation of culture, and how "these tasks are just as meaningful as events and realizations marked by dominant discourses" (Riley-Mukavetz 120). These concepts dovetail powerfully within Chicana feminists' perspectives of Third Space—a discursive, imaginative, and/or material space where marginalized people "refuse to accept mainstream definitions of themselves and insist that they establish and affirm their own identity" through discursive and material practice (Flores 146). Therefore, I also employ a Chicana feminist term, "rhetoric of difference," which Flores describes as a rhetoric which breaks with "mainstream discourse and espousing self – and group – created discourse" in order for "marginalized groups [to] establish themselves as different from stereotyped perceptions and different from dominant culture" (Flores 145).

As I study how LPP's daily practices formulate a culture—a Third Space—of resistance and self-defining, I draw from works which value how everyday life rhetorically forms communities and, in turn, a distinct culture ("The Cultural Rhetorics Theory Lab"; de Certeau; Riley-Mukavetz; Bratta and Powell). I conclude this chapter with a discussion about how these everyday practices at the shelter are *rasquache* rhetorics that manifest "from a sociocultural imperative to recycle, upcycle, make do, and make new meaning through whatever available bits and pieces" in order to exercise subversive politics (Medina-López).

In what follows, I focus on three alternative narratives that clients at LPP composed through routines: "I am useful"; "I have a (temporary) family"; and "I am patriotic without citizenship." These three narratives push back against the persistent narratives of loss and perpetual exclusion that overshadow the experience of people who seek asylum.

Crocheting: I Am Useful

The predominant alternative narrative clients offered centered on their own usefulness while at LPP; often clients and volunteers were able to find their worth as they engaged with "things" within the everyday routines at the shelter. Feminist new materialist Jane Bennett describes things as not merely objects but "vivid entities not entirely reducible to the contexts to which (human) subjects set them" (5). For example, Esther, Ayana, Timotheo, Yazmin, and Santos were clients who commented on their routine work in collaboration with and the formation of things—gardens, fences, hats, or baked goods—to help support the shelter's rhythm. Esther shared her photo, "Crochet" (Figure 5.1), and explained the routine to me this way: "on Tuesdays, they are teaching us [how to crochet hats]—well, as long as you want to learn. I am very interested in learning because, I don't know, it might help me someday when I go back to my country. It's very interesting." While crocheting has been part of LPP's rhythm for many years ("Hands of Love"; "My Fourth Visit"), I'm interested in tracing the routine of crocheting to understand how such an everyday activity works as a material assemblage to compose a "rhetoric of difference" (Flores 143).

On a basic level, the act of crocheting with others can be interpreted as a type of relational and community-based cultural production, referred to as a "constellative practice" which "emphasizes the degree to which knowledge is never built by individuals but is, instead, accumulated through collective practices within specific communities," that works to compose and perpetuate culture (Bratta and Powell). In other words, as people create, work, and produce things as a collective, they are able to compose a shared understanding of values and roles for themselves and the group. Understanding culture

Figure 5.1 "Crochet" shows a purple crochet loom full of olive-green yarn on top of Esther's lap. Photo by Esther.

formation this way prioritizes routine acts as powerful ways to daily reinforce, revise, or resist individual and group identity by privileging the "thereness" or dailiness of life (Riley-Mukavetz).

Additionally, because such routine work, like crocheting, is done in concert with material objects, such as yarn, hooks, scissors, and tape measures, we can read the agency of such matter within culture formation. In fact, Bennett describes how as we notice the agency of objects, we realize their "thing power" or "the curious ability of inanimate things to animate, to act, to produce effects dramatic and subtle" (6). All of these "things" work in concert with humans to make meaning. The Cultural Rhetorics Theory Lab describes plainly, "people make things (texts, baskets, performances), people make relationships, people make culture." At its core, then, the act of crocheting in a group positions Esther as one agent within the assemblage of culture formation at LPP. Such a material assemblage, afforded by the rhetorical network of LPP, helps Esther partake in what Bennett describes as "distributed agency" or the theory that "an actant never really acts alone. Its efficacy or agency always depends on the collaboration, cooperation, or interactive interference of many bodies and forces" (21). And as Esther partakes of this assemblage, she enhances her own individual and group power. As Bennett explains, power "becomes distributed across an ontologically heterogeneous field, rather than being a capacity localized in a human body or in a collective produced (only) by human efforts" (23).

In other words, Esther is supported by the shelter because the space welcomes her as a valuable and agentive member of the network (consisting of humans and non-human things) through the routine of crocheting.

In fact, because the hats Esther and the group created were sold to help offset clients' travel expenses, the routine has an even more layered effect in Esther's perspective of her own agency. Esther describes her assemblage/work within the community plainly yet powerfully: "if they help you, you work together with them to return that help." While this "help" and "work" may sound obligatory, none of the clients spoke about an obligation to work at the shelter. Instead, many clients spoke of the satisfaction they found in their work as an agentive actant within the community. Now, Esther's narrative of her routine act of crocheting and productivity can work to contrast the victim narrative that predominantly surrounds her life as a displaced person (Steimel, "Refugees"). For example, Esther's interest in learning to crochet in these weekly gatherings directly correlated with her desire to invest in her country of origin and be useful to her family who remained there. After she described her weekly crocheting routine, she added:

> [If] God allows us or would allow us to remain here, well, [laughs] we would always say that the first thing was—as long as we had a decent job, well—we would always say that we would send money back to [country of origin] to build a house. That was the first thing we all wanted. And to continue studying.
>
> (Esther)

Esther shared that she had to leave her youngest daughter with family in her country of origin; thus, her comments about sending money home, possibly earned through her crocheting skills, reveal how such everyday tasks, such as creating hats, afford Esther a measure of agency in her future and identity as a resourceful woman who can provide for her family. Indeed, bringing the "material conditions faced by many [marginalized groups]" to the forefront in this way "forces [us] to see those who might otherwise remain invisible. By elevating the everyday, Chicana feminists empower those who might otherwise go unnoticed" (Flores 148). Such an assemblage of utility and culture formation is empowering to clients because it allows them to foster a narrative of resistance or a "rhetoric of difference" about their stereotypical role as "victim." In many ways, Esther is crocheting—or creating—material links to her family in her home country with this activity, as she views the act of crocheting as an economically profitable act.

Esther's crocheting is similar to the crafting done by The Red Tent Women's Initiative. Feminist rhetorics scholar Jill McCracken and colleagues describe how The Red Tent facilitates sewing and embroidery within a Florida jail in which they create "crafts that symbolize their life experiences, personal goals, and successes" (178). Through the act of making, the women are able to "disrupt the helpless victim or criminal roles often associated with people who are or were formerly incarcerated" (McCracken et al. 179).

Shifting labels is a work of activism, which is why the work of crafting for activist causes is labeled "craftivism." Additionally, new materialist rhetorics scholar Leigh Gruwell writes about craft agency and craftivism in her book *Making Matters, Crafts, Ethics, and New Materialist Rhetorics*, in which she argues that for marginalized communities, crafting "can foster social ties, which can then crystalize into more durable activist networks that advocate for and even create change" (Gruwell 15).

In this way, Esther's crocheting routine functions as a unique semi-private performance of value, utility, and agency. As a collective, the group uses crocheting to name or "mark themselves" (Powell, *Identity*, 173) as useful. As an individual, crocheting—the very physicality of it—may also work as a necessary distraction for Esther. Such a distraction not only empowers clients to avoid dwelling on themselves as victims but, for a few, also helps them consider their futures. For example, Timotheo communicated that he wishes there was "something more substantial for [clients] to do" while at the shelter to aid in distraction:

> [I wish there was] something that would distract them emotionally while contributing to [the shelter], like when we made all those [crocheted hats] for [a shelter fundraiser]. At the same time, they were being distracted … and the money that was made was used to help those people when they left—they were given that money when they left—it was like savings they got to take with them.
>
> (Timotheo)

Here, Timotheo echoes Esther's perspective about the give and take of support at the shelter; his idea for a partnership with the shelter clients to begin micro-businesses is an idea grounded in the belief that people seeking asylum are productive and self-sufficient, essentially revising the victim narrative that displaced people bear. What is more, Timotheo and Esther's respective plans for using the craft of crocheting align with Gruwell's description of craftivism: which "always makes visible how power circulates—and can be challenged—through the material. In craftivism, materiality matters, as bodies, tools, spaces, and objects work together to intervene in political struggles and inequitable relationships, with the ultimate goal of remaking a more ethical, just world" (61).

Both Timotheo and Esther see crocheting as more than a distraction; instead, they understand the act of creating material objects as an avenue to promote change in the daily lives of marginalized people. However, the crocheting group at LPP is predominately made of clients with only a few volunteers, so the crafts are created by the very community it serves, thereby complicating the savior/victim binary commonly associated with humanitarian or activist work. The shelter, then, uses crocheting to resist the victim narrative not only in collaborating with clients to be productive through making hats but also using the revenue from hats to assist the clients themselves. Through this material assemblage, they are able to compose stories about themselves which highlight their dynamic experiences with displacement based on their daily life at the shelter.

Housework: I Have a (Temporary) Family

Another alternative narrative that clients tell about themselves while at LPP focuses on their connection to the shelter as a type of surrogate family, and this is performed primarily through housework. Such a story effectively counters the mainstream narrative of loss that hovers over people seeking asylum. For example, within Timotheo's perspective about how he supports others at the shelter, he emphasizes LPP as a family. As a staff member who was once a client and has since been granted asylum, Timotheo offers the following counsel to clients within LPP:

> Well, laughing, talking, making their lives a little easier, giving them advice—not like an expert but like someone who's been through something similar. It's like saying, "We have to keep moving forward. God is with us, and this is a process. This isn't our country." … [I offer] support as a friend, not as a professional. Telling them to trust in God. We need to have faith in God, and we have to support each other. If there are people that came here without family, I tell them, "I came here without family, and I've gotten through it." I know I've suffered because I've been—I came by myself, but thank God, now I have [the shelter] who is like my family.
>
> (Timotheo)

In his hypothetical advice to clients, I interpret Timotheo's emphasis on the absence of family and citizenship/national belonging as a way to compose and identify those at LPP as a surrogate family. Indeed, the clients I spoke to described that the companionship and familial atmosphere were grounded in collaborative housework, like cleaning and cooking, which I expand on in this section. Such a strategy aligns with Third Space practices posited by Chicana feminists:

> Through their recognition and subsequent rejection of stereotypes, their reordering of significant experiences to include the daily activities of many Chicanas and Mexican Americans, their celebration of their culture, and their redefinition of family, Chicana feminists proclaim their identity and create for themselves not only a space but a home in which they can overcome feelings of isolation and alienation.
>
> (Flores 145)

Often this act of non-binary self-definition and claims to home and family is done for survival; for example, when considering LPP as a Third Space, we understand that the need to establish home and family is a reaction to the impossibility of "going home" or reuniting with loved ones. Anzaldúa responds to such inhibitions: "And if going home is denied me then I will have to stand and claim my space, making a new culture—*una cultura mestiza*—with my own lumber, my own bricks and mortar and my own feminist architecture" (44). In other words, clients at LPP understand that the shelter may function as a temporary family during the in-betweens as they face family loss and separation.

I argue that one facet of "feminist architecture" which LPP clients employ is domestic chores, like cooking and cleaning. Esther, who took many photos of the kitchen and dining area, was able to capture a moment (with Timotheo's help) which explicitly showcases her performing routine cooking duties, as the background wall contains a sign in the dining room which states, "many cultures, one family in God" (Figure 5.2).

Such a direct and clear message is displayed while the group cooks, eats, and cleans together on a daily basis. While not all clients read English, and therefore may not be able to absorb the direct argument of the sign, the poster still demonstrates an ideology at play in this space: despite the differences of those who arrive, all clients are united as a "family." The religious underpinning of their kinship is often communicated in many ways at the shelter (even seen in Timotheo's above comments); however, my focus here is how cooking and cleaning are the quotidian acts which demonstrate, perpetuate, and mark the LPP community as "one family."

For example, Yazmin and Ayana both shared how the kitchen space is a place where they feel supported by the community because it offers distraction and enjoyment. Yazmin shares, "sometimes we come here to make desserts, cookies, so here, I feel distracted, and I like to cook, that is, make cookies and stuff" (Figure 5.3).

Ayana described her experience in the kitchen this way: "Well, there, I love it [laughs] because I kill a lot of time there. There is always something to do in the kitchen, and I always help the cook. Every time he calls me to help him peel potatoes, to peel carrots, to put out the bread, so these are ways, one, to help and also a way to—pass the time. That is, to keep me busy with something."

Ayana sees cooking as offering a double benefit for her; first, it helps her to connect with the cook, and secondly, she is able to combat the mental turmoil of her persecution/victimhood by keeping busy. Previous work from Lilja Ingvarsson and colleagues as well as Halleh Ghorashi et al. demonstrates how normalcy and routine provide mental distraction to people seeking asylum. In addition, the study by Ingvarsson and colleagues shows how routine contributed to feelings of productivity and self-worth as well as opportunities for meaningful relationships within their new communities. Those in this study who were able to gain employment or volunteer expressed feelings of "self-respect, independence, contributing to society, and belonging" (Ingvarsson et al. 420);

Figure 5.2 "Kitchen 2" depicts the back of Esther in the LPP kitchen separating cut fruit in bowls. Photo by Esther.

Figure 5.3 The kitchen located in Casa Carolina. Photo by Yazmin.

however, another crucial, albeit often neglected, benefit was the mental distraction and focus that such activities provide.

Ayana's situation perhaps exemplifies the layered need for such a distraction most poignantly. Although she had been at the shelter for about a month, she hadn't filed an official asylum application, and for various reasons beyond her control, her process was at what she described as a "dead stop." This halt compelled her to avoid planning for the future, which includes reuniting with her son and pursuing an education. Instead, Ayana keeps herself engaged with housework to distract herself from the precarity of her situation and the emotional pain of her persecution, journey, and family separation. She explains, "I'm always doing this and doing that. I'm cleaning because I've been told that it's important to keep my mind occupied because, when I'm here in my bedroom, all I can think about is that I want to leave, that I want to be with my son." She also adds, "I always say, one has to try to keep one's mind occupied in something because, if not, it's hard to be here seven days a week. That is, it's not easy. Even though you may have peace and your spaces, you're always thinking about your family, about your case."

Interestingly, Ayana's need to keep her mind off her biological family prompted her to engage in housework with her LPP family; thus, she revised her "loss" narrative through cleaning alongside her surrogate family at LPP. Similar to Ayana, the displaced people involved in Ingvarsson and colleagues' study "even spent extra hours … cooking, in order to pass time" (420). Such acts align with de Certeau's tactics of agency and resistance, especially in that such routine enables clients at LPP to combat the feelings of precariousness in material ways. In de Certeau's perspective, everyday people use "tactics" in order to exercise agency at the right time, "always watching for opportunities that must be seized 'on the wing'" (xix). Tactics are juxtaposed with "strategies" or methodical power plays from those in dominance. A strategy refers to the enveloping structures of the dominant establishments, such as government, education, and religious organizations, and their ideological and material ends, such as to make money or enlist followers. Tactics, on the other hand, are the ways in which individuals are able to resist dominance through unplanned, yet effective, enactments of freedom in situations which open an opportunity for such enactments.

In de Certeau's second volume of *The Practice of Everyday Life*, the authors Luce Giard and Pierre Mayol employ de Certeau's ideas about tactics to study kitchens and cooking in particular. Giard's research in French kitchens highlights how "the gestures, objects, and words that live in the ordinary nature of a simple kitchen also have so much importance" because kitchens are a place where an individual has the ability to "seize power over one part of oneself" (Giard 213). This is achieved through what Giard refers to as "doing-cooking" or the acts of "manipulating raw materials, of organizing, combining, modifying, ad inventing" (152). In this way, Esther, Yazmin, and Ayana are able to "become producers of their own little 'cultural industry'" of the kitchens of LPP in order to connect and find their place in their surrogate families while they stay there (Giard 254). Indeed, Giard underscores how sharing the food we cook through eating together "make[s] concrete one of the specific modes of relation between a person and the world, thus forming one of the fundamental landmarks in space-time" (Giard 183). Cooking and eating, then, are powerful routines which help create surrogate families and designated roles in a temporary space.

Another domestic chore that works as a tactic of the agency is cleaning; Ayana described how she uses the weekly cleaning schedule to feel connected to her shared bedroom (Figure 5.4), even a sense of ownership of the space. She explains about her bedroom: "It feels like my space. I know it's not my house, but it feels like my space. And I take that very seriously. Once a week, we have to clean, and I take it as if it's my own house. It just feels like my space."

The feelings of attachment are mirrored in her roommate Yazmin's description of the space:

> Well, being here, I don't feel so alone because several of us sleep here, so before going to sleep, we talk, and well, then I fall asleep, but I don't feel alone, like if I had my own room. Instead, I feel like I have companionship, and it's comforting because, before falling asleep, we talk and snack on something, so it feels more—what's the word—endure. It's easier to endure the days.
>
> (Yazmin)

Figure 5.4 "*Nuestra Habitación*"/"Our Room" shows a women's dorm in Casa Carolina with bright blue walls and single beds with bright bedding. Photo by Ayana.

As Yazmin and Ayana work together to routinely clean their shared bedroom, clients at the shelter are able to position themselves within LPP and compose new stories which work to detract from their feelings of precariousness. But instead of simply being distracted to avoid their painful narratives of loss, the routines help clients negotiate new stories about themselves. As explained in Chapter 3, Reynolds' *Geographies of Writing* focuses on "reimagining composing as spatial, material, and visual" and "to understanding the sociospatial construction of difference" (3). In other words, composing is located and local, dependent upon on-the-ground contexts, seen in clients' feelings of ownership of a space based on their routine care for it. For example, in her book, *A Place to Stand: Politics & Persuasion in a Working Class Bar*, cultural rhetorician Julie Lindquist, in an exemplary illustration of methodology and positioning of "there-ness," explores the narrative and argumentative positioning of staff and regulars of a local bar within middle America. Lindquist argues that culture is based on shared practices which are forged through "local formations that emerge from the tense relation between the exigencies of particular sites of immediate, embodied experience and the larger political economy" (Lindquist 5). What I gain from Lindquist here is that clients are seizing an opportunity to revise their stories of loss (larger political economy) through their "particular sites of immediate, embodied experience" (cleaning their bedroom). Through the simple and shared routines of domestic chores, the clients are able to gradually formulate familial bonds which resist the narrative of family separation, even if this narrative is understood and circulated only among themselves.

The act of claiming their bedroom as a space which feels like their own relates to arguments from cultural rhetorician André Brock. In his essay, "'Who do you think you are?': Race, Representation, and Cultural Rhetorics in Online Spaces," Brock stretches the idea of located rhetoric to offer insight into how marginal communities have a unique sense of how space and place afford and constrain rhetorical possibilities for Black communities:

> I would argue [...] that due to environmental segregation in the United States, that Black people have always had to make do with whatever geographic location they were allowed to occupy. Thus the stoop, the porch, the corner, the store, and the aforementioned barber and beauty salons all became places where Black men and women could philosophize, sympathize, and enjoy each other's company. This is not to say that Blacks did not conduct "third place" activities in churches, bars, Masonic temples, fraternity/sorority houses, or country clubs! I have mentioned more transient locations such as "the corner" to point out that even in a cultural milieu that fears congregations of Black people, Black people have always found time and space to discuss (with humor and with wisdom) what it means to be Black.
>
> (Brock 33)

Brock's argument provokes a curiosity about how "shared cultural experiences (and the narrative processes and products of these experiences) are linked to material conditions," or "what happens at the local level manifests what is structural and systemic" (Lindquist 5). In other words, the on-the-ground, material, and embodied daily experiences of the community, with things, matter, and space, are rhetorical negotiations between the present sociocultural conditions of the time and the cultural-rhetorical pushback to such conditions (Lindquist 5). At LPP, then, clients are able to negotiate the hegemonic narratives in which they exist while also composing rhetorical resistance to such narratives. Like Lindquist, I see value in observing the quotidian, material objects available within a community which impact their realities.

Another example comes from Yazmin who emphasized the importance of the laundry area (Figure 5.5), where she worked "together" with clients to complete this chore:

> Every weekend, on Saturday, we all clean [the shelter]. We wash, we clean, and there is the laundry room. Mostly on weekends, we all gather our clothes, and we wash, and—well, we go together. We all go together. One washes. One gathers the clothes. One takes the clothes, so you can see the help we give and the way we share our chores, the women we share a room with.
>
> (Yazmin)

Figure 5.5 "Laundry" captures the path to the laundry buildings and the small laundry buildings in the distance surrounded by green space. Photo by Yazmin.

Yazmin's emphasis on togetherness and collaboration through shared chores in the laundry area demonstrates the material assemblage of routine. The story she tells here is not just about cleaning clothes but about the culture that is constituted from such routine, especially in that cooking and cleaning help foster a shared responsibility of a space.

In the end, such activities of shared living translate to home, and Alex's visualizations of LPP as a home are particularly insightful. The few photos he offered demonstrate themes of family and routine. "Housework" (Figure 5.6) and "Play Process" (Figure 5.7) both capture scenes which demonstrate the family-friendly environment at the shelter. This feeling of home, Alex describes, is important to him because he sees it as an inspiration for him to continue moving forward in his process. Additionally, seeing families together offers a hope that is seldom seen in asylum contexts. In fact, even though Alex was trying to find another shelter outside of Texas so that his case could be heard in a more liberal-leaning court, he laments that he would be leaving behind the many families at LPP. Alex's visualizations represent what "normal" means to him, especially family routines; for example, it is normal for a child to play alongside their parents; it is normal for a parent to do housework and care for children; and it is normal to have spaces that afford conversation, rest, and connection. Alex's images may be unusual in the common narrative surrounding asylum because

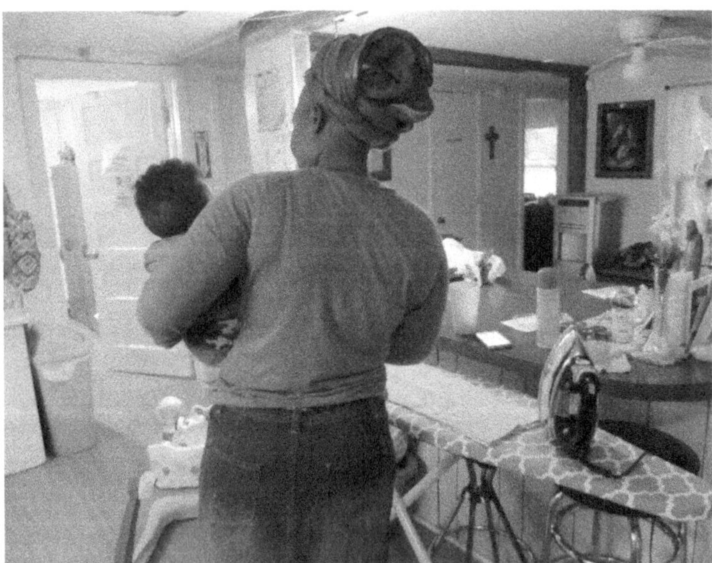

Figure 5.6 "Housework" captures a mother taking a break from ironing to carry her child in the kitchen within Casa Carolina. Photo by Alex.

Figure 5.7 "Play Process" shows an overhead view of a child playing near his mother with toys scattered on the floor of Casa Carolina. Photo by Alex.

such places and spaces associated with asylum are constraining, depressing, and lonely; thus, LPP is functioning as a Third Space where clients are able to compose alternative rhetorics which offer hope to one another.

What is more, asylum processes in the U.S. conjure images of family separation and loss. In contrast, the images Alex offers are focused on people and everyday activities and spaces that bring marginalized communities to the center. Studying the daily and local practices of the shelter provides a decolonial perspective that highlights how commonplace activity and "there-ness" (Riley-Mukavetz) of those who dwell within a space/place are just as impacting to constituting a culture as prevailing perspectives and discourses of asylum experience. As Riley-Mukavetz explains, instead of narrowly defining culture solely on "any combination of race, ethnicity, gender, or class," culture may also be understood "by the spaces/places people share, how people organize themselves, and how they practice shared beliefs" (109).

Singing: I Am Patriotic without Citizenship

Yet another alternative narrative I observed at the shelter was patriotism without citizenship. This narrative is messy in that citizenship is a highly contested term, especially within the shelter. To put it simply, citizenship as a status and label "reifies the coloniality of power … to subalternize racialized knowledges" (Ribero 33). Perhaps this is seen most clearly in Benjamin's perspective of his assigned reading during language classes. Because of his language proficiency, the staff gave him a book to study with more challenging readings, *Future U.S. Citizens* (Lynn). For Benjamin, this book was a hurtful reminder that he had been denied asylum, and his "withholding of removal" status was only temporary permission to stay in the U.S. without any pathway to hope or dignity for long-term resettlement and acceptance that citizenship entails.

> [The staff] say to me, 'come learn this.' This book they give me, you see? *Future U.S. Citizens*. Is that for me? I will learn this book. I will read it. But who can give me this "U.S. Citizenship?" I don't have any court process. I don't have nothing. Even if I go to court also, again, the results, I don't know. You understand me? But I'm studying this. For what purpose? What is the reason? There is no reason. There is no purpose to learn this because nobody give you [future].
>
> (Benjamin)

While the staff's intentions may have been to provide Benjamin with more stimulating activity, Benjamin's fleeting U.S. allowance to stay was in painful tension with the book's title and purpose. Benjamin's thoughtful reaction demonstrates how citizenship is positioned "always on the horizon yet forever out of reach for racialized Others in the United States" (Ribero 39). Indeed, the book works as a material reminder, in its title and readings (which are often read aloud in a group) of the perpetual exclusion he has faced in the U.S. What is more, the book plays into the ideology that the nation-state is the exclusive pathway to agency.

Despite this painful narrative of exclusion which Benjamin experienced, clients spoke about singing as a way to perform patriotism even though they lacked citizenship. At the start of the language and U.S. culture classes, which run for 4 hours a day in morning and afternoon 2-hour blocks (see Appendix B), clients sing for about 10 minutes. The morning class begins with music, and to boost participation, volunteers hand out lyric sheets as well as small instruments, like maracas, tambourines, and even small hand drums. Most clients I have observed seem to enjoy the singing and are enthusiastic about beginning class this way. Although the class is meant for adults, parents will usually sit with their children as they clap, sing, and read the lyrics together. Sister, who teaches and oversees the English classes, will typically play on her guitar or a CD player a mixture of patriotic songs, such as "God Bless America" or "My Country 'tis of Thee," as well as songs with religious themes like "He's Got the Whole World in His Hands." Often, Sister will change the words to such songs to personalize the music. For example, in the latter song, Sister may change the lyrics from "the whole world" to "La Posada." In fact, in each subsequent verse of this particular song, she routinely narrows geographically from "whole world" to the particular city the shelter is located, then to "La Posada," and finally to "mamas and babies," in addition to the original lyrics of "you and me, sister/brother."

By changing the lyrics, Sister gradually and profoundly locates clients within the rhetorical network of LPP through the client's own collaborative voices. In her published talk, "Notes toward a Politics of Location," feminist poet Adrienne Rich describes how as a young woman she would position herself in similar ways as she addressed letters to friends. Beginning with her physical street address, she would add a widening location, such as her state, country, continent, hemisphere, "The Earth," and finally "The Universe." By doing so, Rich contextualized herself within the overlapping networks and rhetorical ecologies in which she existed: "you could see your own house as a tiny fleck on an ever widening landscape, or as the center of it all from which the circles expanded into the infinite unknown" (212). By changing the lyrics to spiritual songs in this way, Sister invites clients to contextualize themselves materially—their bodies, their children's bodies, and their stories—at "the center of it all" or "in His hands." This singing, then, begins clients' days and prepares them for the performance of narratives of resistance to perceptions in which they are marginalized and perpetually foreign through their lack of citizenship.

Of course, the external purpose of the singing is to help clients learn English; Esther remarks how "we sing every day when we come to class, and I like it because, well, that is how I learn to break things apart because I learn faster through songs." Esther's untitled photo of the annotated copy of the lyrics to the song, "God Bless America," depicts what she calls "her favorite hymn" that she received in language class (Figure 5.8). Esther spoke about how the song's written translation from English to Spanish provided an opportunity for her to not only sing along but also understand the song's meaning, which she values a great deal. Esther's assemblage with this lyric sheet, the translated words, as well as the guitar and fellow clients' voices demonstrates how she is materially able to resist narratives of being an "outsider" by performing patriotism without citizenship in her native language. Indeed, in Bruno Latour's *Reassembling the Social*, he describes how "things might authorize, allow, afford, encourage, permit, suggest, influence, block, render possible, forbid, and so on" (89). In other words, the efficacy of Esther's learning, understanding, and reveling in such a patriotic song demonstrates how effectively the "things" at LPP work together with her to affect change (Gries et al. 87) about the stories told about her as a woman seeking asylum.

Moreover, Esther mentioned that the lyric sheet in this photo was given to her with handwritten translations already on it. The shelter prides itself on green practices, so re-using the lyric sheet is unsurprising, but what is enlightening is how Esther inherited the lyric sheet with another client's writing, perspective, and agency to write the lyrics of a patriotic song in their own native language. Such is another layer of the assemblage in which Esther is embedded which affords her permission to enact stories of resistance.

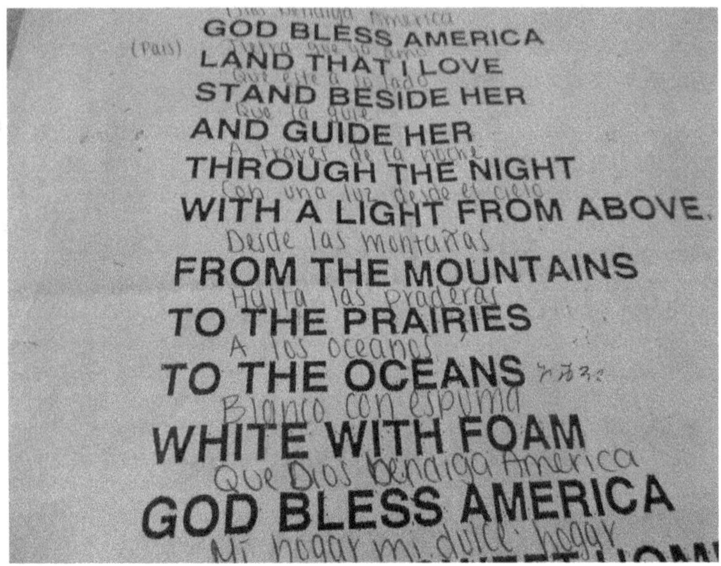

Figure 5.8 A picture of a lyrics sheet of the song "God Bless America" printed in English and the Spanish translations handwritten in ink underneath each line.

Of course, Esther's routine of singing such a patriotic song calls to mind arguments from *Who Sings the Nation State?* by Judith Butler and Gayatri Chakravorty Spivak. In this work, Butler and Spivak crucially explore "what makes for a non-nationalist or counter-nationalist mode of belonging" (58–59), but they do so primarily through analyzing a very public, intentional, and easily recognizable performance of resistance in which undocumented Latin American immigrants in southern California publicly gathered to sing the U.S. national anthem in Spanish. In contrast, Esther's singing is not occurring in a broad protest; it is a quiet routine in her day, intimate and thoughtful. Such an act is quintessential to Third Space life, as described by Flores, who argues that there is an overemphasis on the public narratives of resistance, especially in that marginalized people have limited access to such powerful public platforms; therefore, for people like those who are seeking asylum, "'private' discourse plays a public role" and "Chicana feminists find … 'private' discourses to be useful rhetorical tools for publicly expressing their private selves" (Flores 145).

Additionally, singing, as a private discourse and routine, may enable clients at LPP liberty to perform other acts of patriotism. In a photo titled, "La Bandera" (Figure 5.9), Esther shared how significant it was for her to raise, lower, and even touch the U.S. flag at the shelter each day, and she spoke directly about what such an act means to her as an immigrant seeking refuge in a

Figure 5.9 "*La Bandera*"/"The Flag" is a photo of the U.S. flag on a flagpole outside Casa Guillermo with a blue sky and clouds in the background.

land that "the world" dreams of being part of. This routine began when Esther took it upon herself to raise the flag one morning when others had forgotten; the same day, no one had lowered it by sunset, so she took the initiative again to finish the job. When the staff noticed this, they informed her that the job was hers from now on, and every day since, the fellow clients will remind her to do it.

> Well, that's the flag. Well, since I've already been here one month, everyday at seven in the morning, it's my job to raise the flag, and then around six-six-thirty—I take it down, and it means a lot to me now that I am in this country. I get very excited because the world dreams about being in this country. It is the dream, and to touch the flag, well, I feel [excited] to be in this country where I've always wanted to be.
>
> (Esther)

In her very embodied and material exchange with a vibrant thing—the U.S. flag—Esther demonstrates how she is drawing from well-established discourses to write herself into the rhetorical ecology of the U.S. asylum system. It is easy to see that this decentering and distribution of agency alters ontological and epistemological assumptions; if objects have agency in and of themselves, like many new materialists, then rhetorical exchanges are not simply dependent on human involvement. As rhetorician Marilyn Cooper describes, "all the characteristics of any individual writer or piece of writing both determine and are determined by the characteristics of all the other writers and writing in the system" (368). In other words, Esther composes herself into a highly recognizable rhetorical "mosaic" (Bennett 22) of patriotism. I see such routine acts as vital because through her embodied "there-ness," Esther has seized an opportunity and uses flag duties as a "tactic" (De Certeau) in conventional ways that represent patriotism. While her acts are surely overtly recognizable and may even be labeled "conventional," perhaps that is what makes them so profound. Esther performs an easily recognizable patriotic act to tell a new story about her own life. In other words, Esther's actions were not necessarily attempting to enact citizenship, but patriotism in ways that many—citizens or not—are able to read.

In light of Benjamin's perspective of struggling to find purpose in reading a book about U.S. citizenship, I interpret Esther's routine performances of patriotism, through singing and flag duties, as messy, not easily categorized as exactly revisionary or resisting the problematic narrative of "unable to achieve the American dream" that follows displaced people (Steimel "Empowerment(s)"). I agree with Chicana feminist Ana Milena Ribero who argues that "citizenship is always already exclusionary and therefore cannot truly be decolonized" and "for people of color, inclusion in citizenship and other dominant forms of belonging requires a reiterative practice of legitimization as they push to be recognized in a framework that depends on exclusion" (Ribero 32). However, by sharing about these everyday experiences, Esther is able to "replace negative images with positive ones" (Flores 147), especially in that she is able to claim certain experiences of patriotism, like routinely calling a country "home" (as in the lyrics in "God Bless America") and taking on flag duties.

***Rasquache* Rhetorics**

Rasquache is a movement popular in Chicanx art, cultural, and literary studies, but hasn't gained much attention in cultural rhetorics. In Kelly Medina-López's article "Rasquache Rhetorics: A Cultural Rhetorics Sensibility," she offers a thorough discussion of *rasquachismo* as a perspective and practice that involves living in the moment and looking for ways to "recycle, upcycle, make do, and make new meaning through whatever available bits and pieces." Medina-López clarifies that *rasquache* rhetorics are not simply about being resourceful and creative; instead exercising *rasquache* includes "an agented choice" and illustrates rhetorical moves that are "political and subversive."

Noticing the new stories that the LPP clients tell about themselves and how those stories manifest, it is clear that they practice "a robust approach to meaning making by allowing [themselves] to pull from the compendium of theories, ideas, experiences, tangible tools, and intangible epistemologies they can access" (Medina-López). When clients tell stories about making hats, cleaning their dorms, or fixing lunch in the shared kitchen, they are acknowledging their own daily struggles for survival and the material ways they accept those realities; however, the stories also testify to the agency they see in their everyday existence.

The stories that clients and staff shared with me about their efforts to survive and thrive demonstrate how they use stories to share their "alternative knowledges" (Medina-López) about displacement. Noticing these alternative knowledges helps us appreciate how much of what mainstream audiences of the Global North see about displacement is filtered through the nation-state and media seeking to reinforce victim/savior binaries. Additionally, these *rasquache* rhetorics work alongside the more traditional protests and advocacy work that is more visible in displacement rhetorics. Valuing the effects of *rasquachismo* can help us re-vision displaced people as those who are receiving help, service, and assistance. We can begin to notice the everyday ways they are able to exercise authority over their own lives outside the shadow of the advocacy group, non-profit agency, or good Samaritan.

Conclusion

This chapter argues that LPP clients are able to develop agency based on shared rhetorics of daily life. By leaning on clients' embodied experiences specific to the shelter, such as crocheting, housework, and singing, I showed how they are able to form a distinct culture which allows them to resist hegemonic stories that overshadow people seeking asylum, such as loss and helplessness. Such stories problematically work to position the nation-state as the exclusive benefactor of rights and agency. Instead of public narratives of asylum which work toward international rights, as discussed in the previous chapter, this chapter focuses on the new stories of agency through normalcy and daily life that clients rhetorically assemble. While these practices do not necessarily focus on writing in a traditional sense, I understand that "all culture is rhetorical" ("The Cultural Rhetorics Theory Lab"). So, the routines I describe here are just as critical to culture formation as traditional forms of rhetoric such as talking, writing, and reading.

And in true cultural rhetorics form, the stories clients tell about how they "endure the days" (Yazmin) showcase how their multivocality may work to change master plots centered on human/nature binaries, which oppress nonhumans, native people, women, and minorities (Conley; Cruikshank; Doyle; Haraway; Plumwood; Sackey; Schmitt).

In other words, client stories about their new normal demonstrate how "narratives are often firmly rooted in the material circumstances of the storyteller," and these stories may work toward social justice (Cruikshank 61). In fact, if the strategies of the nation-state are to present people seeking asylum as a problem to be solved, then the tactics of the clients at LPP are a subversive response to such a narrative. By showcasing the normalcy and routines of shelter life, clients demonstrate their humanity that may be more relatable than narratives of family separation, homelessness, and statelessness.

What is more, these tactics are constellating a culture that is located, material and embodied, rooted in "there-ness" (Riley-Mukavetz) in order to create a home where they take initiative to self-define, group, plan, and choose. As clients told me about their new normal and their routine at the shelter, I began to understand that they had fresh stories to tell about themselves, different from the public narratives of asylum which constitute so much of their identity in high-stakes claims for permission to belong in very public ways. In contrast, their stories of routine allow them to make meaning through agentive practice or tactics which work against the hegemonic stories of asylum that homogenize individuals in the asylum process. Such pushback is unique, not only in that it is a hallmark of differential consciousness as articulated by Chicana feminists, but it is also noteworthy in that such rhetorics do not rely on public resistance, such as demonstrations or protests which are often not accessible to marginalized groups. What this means is that while cleaning or crocheting starkly contrasts with more public enactments of agency, such as protests or marches, such routines should not be discounted in their efficacy to unite a community to (re)vision the hegemonic discourse surrounding them. In fact, within a Third Space, Chicana feminists argue, routine experiences "are given the same worth as the traditionally white-valued 'exceptional experiences" (Flores 147).

In the next chapter, I expand on the role of this work toward social justice and advocacy. I especially consider the need for advocacy initiatives to connect clients' lives to the wider ecologies and materiality which affects their everyday lives.

References

Anzaldúa, Gloria. *Borderlands/La Frontera: The New Mestiza*. Aunt Lute Books, 1987.

Bennett, Jane. *Vibrant Matter: A Political Ecology of Things*. Duke University Press, 2010.

Bratta, Phil and Malea Powell. "Introduction to the Special Issue: Entering the Cultural Rhetorics Conversations." *Enculturation*, 2016, http://enculturation.net/entering-the-cultural-rhetorics-conversations.

Brock, André. "'Who do you think you are?': Race, Representation, and Cultural Rhetorics in Online Spaces." *Poroi*, vol. 6, no. 1, 2009, pp. 15–35, https://doi.org/10.13008/2151-2957.1013.

Butler, Judith and Gayatri Chakravorty Spivak. *Who Sings the Nation State?: Language, Politics, Belonging*. Seagull Books, 2007.

Conley, Paige A. "Strategically Negotiating Essence: Zitkála-Šá's Ethos as Activist." Ryan, Myers & Jones, pp. 173–94.

Cooper, Marilyn M. "The Ecology of Writing." *College English*, vol. 48, no. 4, 1986, pp. 364–75.

Cruikshank, Julie. *Do Glaciers Listen? Local Knowledge, Colonial Encounters, and Social Imagination*. UBC Press, 2005.

De Certeau, Michele. *The Practice of Everyday Life*. The University of California Press, 2011.

Doyle, Julie. "Seeing the Climate? The Problematic Status of Visual Evidence in Climate Change Campaigning." *Ecosee: Image, Rhetoric, Nature*, edited by S. I. Dobrin and Sean Morey, SUNY Press, 2009, pp. 279–98.

Flores, Lisa A. "Creating Discursive Space through a Rhetoric of Difference: Chicana Feminists Craft a Homeland." *Quarterly Journal of Speech*, vol. 82, no. 2, 1996, pp. 142–56, *Routledge*.

Gale, Peter. "The Refugee Crisis and Fear: Populist Politics and Media Discourse." *Journal of Sociology*, vol. 40, 2004, pp. 321–40.

Ghorashi, Halleh, et al. "Unexpected Agency on the Threshold: Asylum Seekers Narrating from an Asylum Seeker Centre." *Current Sociology*, vol. 66, no. 3, 2018, pp. 373–91. *Sage*, doi: 10.1177/0011392117703766.

Gries, Laurie, et al. "New Materialisms, Networks, and Humanities Research." *Networked Humanities: Within and Without the University*, edited by Jeff Rice and Brian McNely, Parlor Press, 2018, pp. 85–104.

Gruwell, Leigh. *Making Matters: Craft, Ethics, and New Materialist Rhetorics*. 1st ed. Utah State University Press, 2022. Web.

"Hands of Love: Client Uses Crocheting Skills to Give Back to La Posada." *La Posada Providencia*. 8 Jan. 2014, https://lppshelter.org/hands-of-love-client-uses-crocheting-skills-to-give-back-to-la-posada/.

Haraway, Donna. *Staying with the Trouble: Making Kin in the Chthulucene*. Duke UP, 2016.

Ingvarsson, Lilja, et al. "'I Want a Normal Life Like Everyone Else': Daily Life of Asylum Seekers in Iceland." *Scandinavian Journal of Occupational Therapy*, vol. 23, no. 6, 2016, pp. 416–424, http://dx.doi.org/10.3109/11038128.2016.1144787.

Lindquist, Julie. *A Place to Stand: Politics & Persuasion in a Working Class Bar*. Oxford UP, 2001.

Lynn, Sarah. *Future U.S. Citizens*. Pearson, 2011.

McCracken, Jill, et al. "Red Tent: Creating Art and Our Lives in Jail through Feminist Rhetorics." *Women's Ways of Making*, edited by Maureen Daly Goggin and Shirley K Rose, University Press of Colorado, 2021, pp. 177–200. *JSTOR*, http://www.jstor.org/stable/j.ctv1kz4gmg.15. Accessed 25 Apr. 2024.

Medina-López, Kelly. "Rasquache Rhetorics: A Cultural Rhetorics Sensibility." *Constellations*, vol. 1, no. 1, 2018. http://constell8cr.com/issue-1/rasquache-rhetorics-a-cultural-rhetorics-sensibility/.

"My Fourth Visit." *La Posada Providencia*. 21 June 2012, https://lppshelter.org/my-fourth-visit-to-la-posada/.

Phillips, Nelson and Cynthia Hardy. "Managing Multiple Identities: Discourse, Legitimacy and Resources in the UK Refugee System." *Organization* vol. 4, 1997, pp. 159–85.

Plumwood, Val. *Feminism and the Mastery of Nature*. Routledge, 1993.

Powell, Katrina M. *Identity and Power in Narratives of Displacement*. Routledge, 2015.

The Cultural Rhetorics Theory Lab (Malea Powell, Daisy Levy, Andrea Riley-Mukavetz, Marilee Brooks-Gillies, Maria Novotny, Jennifer Fisch-Ferguson). "Our Story Begins Here: Constellating Cultural Rhetorics Practices." *Enculturation: A Journal of Rhetoric, Writing, And Culture*, vol. 18, no. 1, 2014, n.p. http://enculturation.net/our-story-begins-here.

Rajaram, Prem Kumar. "Humanitarianism and Representations of the Refugee." *Journal of Refugee Studies*, vol. 15, no. 3, 2002, pp. 247–64. Oxford UP.

Reynolds, Nedra. *Geographies of Writing: Inhabiting Places and Encountering Difference*. Southern Illinois UP, 2004.

Ribero, Ana Milena. "Citizenship." *Decolonizing Rhetoric & Composition Studies*, edited by Iris D. Ruiz and Raul Sánchez, Palgrave Macmillan, 2019, pp. 31–45.

Riley-Mukavetz, Andrea M. "Towards a Cultural Rhetorics Methodology: Making Research Matter with Multi-generational Women from the Little Traverse Bay Band." *Rhetoric, Professional Communication and Globalization*, vol. 5, no. 1, 2014. pp. 108–25.

Sackey, Donnie Johnson. "Tracing ecologies of writing," *2011 IEEE International Professional Communication Conference*, Cincinnati, 2011, pp. 1–6, doi: 10.1109/IPCC.2011.6087188.

Schmitt, Casey R. "Invoking the Ecological Indian: Rhetoric, Culture, and the Environment." *Voice and Environmental Communication*, edited by J. Peeples and S. Depoe. Palgrave Macmillan, 2014, pp. 66–87.

Steimel, Sarah J. "Negotiating Refugee Empowerment(s) in Resettlement Organizations." *Journal of Immigrant & Refugee Studies*, vol. 15, no. 1, 2017, pp. 90–107. *Sage*, doi: 10.1080/15562948.2016.1180470.

Steimel, Sarah J. "Refugees as People: The Portrayal of Refugees in American Human Interest Stories." *Journal of Refugee Studies*, vol. 23, no. 2, 2010, pp. 219–37. *Sage*, doi: 10.1093/jrs/feq019.

6 The Long Path Out through Advocacy-Building

Each time I volunteered at the La Posada Providencia (LPP), I slowly drove upon a long, paved path that is the only road in or out of the property (Figure 6.1). During my time as a volunteer, I drove over this path many times. In my own car, I would usually head from the shelter to pick up my daughters from school where they were safe, and then we would head home, to share time together with my husband in our own home. My path out was when I would usually consider both the balance of mobility and stability (or privilege) that shapes my life. Considering my own privilege after spending time with people

Figure 6.1 "Driveway" captures a long, paved driveway at the entrance of the LPP property surrounded by green space and a palm tree. Photo by Ayana.

DOI: 10.4324/9781003349693-6

facing such uncertainty often brought several emotions at once like guilt, hope, and gratitude.

Through my steady volunteer work and scholarship at LPP, I have developed "the habit" of what Jacquelin Jones Royster describes as "caring as a rhetorician." Such an awareness includes "becoming sensitized for the first time to a fuller understanding of [the] uniqueness" of the relationship between materiality and rhetoric in the lives of those at LPP (258). While I was initially disturbed by these feelings because the LPP clients' precarity "grates against" my own stable life (Anzaldúa 25), I found that caring about the LPP community prompted me to return and drive along this same path, week after week, month after month, year after year. My privilege and position as an ally also made me consider how I would exit the project when that time came. I was certain that part of my path *out* would include building initiatives that motivate partners of advocacy to take the path *into* the community and learn about the nuanced rhetorical ecologies in which the people of LPP are embedded.

Indeed, I was drawn to this project because I see LPP as a rhetorical network, and the variety of stories displaced people tell about themselves is influenced by the rhetorical ecology—a varied and shifting context of narratives, events, people, materials, and policies—that is the U.S. asylum system. I used this project to answer my research questions about LPP's networked position within the wider rhetorical ecology of the U.S. asylum system and how such interconnection affords, constrains, perpetuates, and critiques hegemonic narratives of asylum experience. In sum, I have argued that LPP operates as an influential "Third Space" for people seeking asylum. Through quotidian practices, the people at the shelter enact distinct shelter rhetorics, or shared rhetorical practices of daily life that both safeguard vulnerabilities and enact agency for individuals within precarious spaces.

Considerations and Challenges

Ironically, the shelter's unique characteristics that afford beneficial shelter rhetorics, such as silence and routine, also created major considerations for my research. Meanwhile, the challenges I faced centered on communicating my findings in ways which satisfied both the ethical standards of working with displaced people's stories and genre norms of writing a book for students and scholars in rhetorical studies.

First, I realize that the routines and daily life experiences the clients described to me are in no way indicative of what is happening in other facilities or shelters in the U.S. What this means is that my work must be read contextually and may limit the implications that others may want to apply to similar spaces where displaced people reside along their journeys. For this reason, I have used a blend of scholarly perspectives, namely, rhetorical ecology and Chicana feminisms, to create my methodological approach, *located-listening*, that is distinct and unique to this space.

As I have described in Chapter 2, I formulated this approach collaboratively within the shelter community in order to better understand from the community members themselves what types of questions were important and meaningful for LPP to ask. But that decision brought its own set of challenges concerning how this project would be able to offer something tangible to the shelter once it was complete. Through this scholarly process, I initially learned that the community was looking to me, the research, and my ties to academia to help support them in everyday ways because the project was tailor-made for them. I admit that this expectation brought a lot of pressure and anxiety, but I learned to balance my own fears by leaning on my colleagues and students to partner with me and the shelter to respond to the knowledge this work was building. I have learned, then, that I can look to the research participants and the local community as experts to help me forge paths toward meaningful advocacy efforts.

Another challenge I faced was writing about this work in the larger field of rhetorical studies. As I worked to contextually listen to the stories and visuals (data), I understood—like others in the field of cultural rhetorics—that labels and codes are incapable (as they should be) of representing the storied lives of those who participated, especially those who are seeking asylum. I struggled with what scholar Linda Tuhiwai Smith describes as "getting the story right" and "telling the story well," especially to the interdisciplinary readers who may read sections of this work (226). What this means is that I had an ethical and personal responsibility to the participants to avoid reducing their stories to smaller labels that may problematically box their experiences in binaries that frustrate understandings of the wider geopolitical rhetorical ecologies they must negotiate; however, I also had a responsibility to write this project with respect to the academic discipline and traditional expectations of the book genre. To help me meet both of those goals, I learned to follow my instincts as a cultural rhetorician and center on stories.

To account for the choices I made, I looked to cultural rhetoricians who, like me, do work within marginalized communities to understand how everyday rhetorical practices reveal underpinning ideologies. Powell and Riley-Mukavetz have, respectively, emphasized the challenges with communicating stories they gather for their research to the field. Riley-Mukavetz explains how her alternative research process of centralizing her participants' stories allows her to "put relationships at the center of research" (112); Malea Powell, in "Listening to Ghosts," echoes Royster and scrutinizes how "[w]e have cut the wholeness of knowledge into little bits, scattered them to the four winds and now begin to reorganize them into categories invented to enable empire by bringing order to chaos and civilization to the savage" (15). To add, I agree with Riley-Mukavetz who warns that cultural rhetoricians are sensitive to such carving and restructuring of knowledge "because it speaks to how we privilege certain types of knowledge over another" (114). For this project, I worked toward embracing the messy and ambivalent rhetorics that are often present in a Third Space; such rhetorics specifically embrace non-binary labels and categories.

A choice I made in my effort to resist segmenting "wholeness of knowledge to little bits" (Powell 15) is to not report my analytical codes in Chapter 2 which outlines my methodology and methods. This choice allowed me to not label/describe/name my participants' stories divorced from the stories themselves. Instead, the *in vivo* codes I used to understand participants' experiences are present within each chapter, such as in a Chapter 4 subheading, "'We learn to endure everything ourselves': Selective silence." My choice to delay reporting my codes within each chapter was important for me in this project, and it is important for me to continue this practice in future work because I want my audiences to listen to stories of displaced people with as much context as possible.

As I explained in Chapter 2, I did not use software to help me code or transcribe data; instead, I listened to the interviews several times, as I sat at my desk, cooked, and jogged. I typed out their words myself over hours of patient listening. I kept my participants' stories in my head, and I wrote reflective blog posts in order to keep the conversation going, allowing my own biases, questions, and frustrations to bubble over. Using a blog to help me organize information as I relistened to interviews allowed *in vivo* coding to remain a cyclical and iterative process, but my emphasis was always on the stories as a whole. This was an experience I could not recreate for my readers, but what I could do was discursively suspend labels or codes like "selective silence" until I was able to fully elaborate with participants' own multi-layered perspectives within subsequent chapters. This was a rhetorical choice I made for this book to help me "tell the story well" (satisfy my academic audience) as well as "get the story right" (provide context about the stories from people at LPP).

Yet another consideration was the fact that speaking to people seeking asylum while they are also clients at LPP limited how and what they were able to share about their daily lives. The more I conducted interviews, the more I realized this; however, I especially considered the implications of my project when someone (client, staff, or volunteer) would choose not to speak to me or when I noted how overwhelmingly positive clients spoke about the space. Their choice to not participate communicated just how precarious LPP is as a site for "outsiders." The people who live and work there may have decided not to participate in order to not jeopardize the stability they had gained, either in their place of refuge, occupations, grant funding, or community support.

While I recognize this reality, I don't see their silence as a "limitation" for this project (although it felt like it each time someone decided not to participate) because I understand more deeply now how displaced people and those who work with them may live with anxiety about being misunderstood, and they may use silence to protect themselves. This is a lesson I have learned about conducting research with marginalized communities specifically. As I detailed in Chapter 4, silence is a distinct shelter rhetoric, and listening to silence resists traditional approaches to rhetoric that center on persuasion. In this way, storytelling at LPP is based on "invitational rhetoric" (Foss and Griffin) that makes space for clients to enact agency through silences. In other words, silence is part of their rhetorical agency. As may be expected, however, I wonder about how the stories that were not told may have contained diverse perspectives about how shelter rhetorics can impact agency and identity for people seeking asylum; at the same time, I understand that no one owes me—or any researcher—their story.

Implications and Recommendations

My recommendations stemming from the implications of my research centralize listening to shelter rhetorics so that people who engage with displacement rhetorics can "highlight the material complexities" of displaced people's stories (Dingo, "Re-Evaluating," 147–8). This approach, referred to as transnational rhetorical literacies, calls for "connecting individual lives, stories, and sufferings with wider systems of historical, cultural, and material local and geopolitics" (Dingo, "Re-Evaluating," 147–8).

Without such context, the literacies we use to engage with asylum narratives may simply participate in the simplistic understanding of forced displacement that perpetuates binaries: "[decontextualized] stories ask readers to become neo-colonizers who merely offer a gaze of recognition without being cognizant of the wider vectors of power that impact these individual [people's] lived experiences" (Dingo, "Macro and Micro," 539).

A practical way to nurture transnational literacies based on my work is to "network [displaced peoples'] stories to wider cultural, political, historical, and economic issues" (Dingo, "Macro and Micro," 540) in the dissemination of my research, especially in the kinds of advocacy work that stem from this study. Indeed, I believe that this project shows the effectiveness of rhetorical ecology theory as part of a blended methodology toward building advocacy initiatives that foster transnational rhetorical literacies. In this way, those who work with displaced people—in governmental/institutional, advocacy/community-engaged learning, or research contexts—will locate insights when we revise and expand our rhetorical data to include the wider rhetorical ecologies in which displaced people must navigate.

In what follows, I directly respond to my three main inquiries for this project that I outlined in Chapter 1:

- How does LPP operate as a rhetorical network within the rhetorical ecology of the U.S. asylum system?
- How does the shelter, as a networked site, afford or constrain the variety of stories people seeking asylum tell about their lived experiences?
- How do the stories produced at the shelter perpetuate or critique the hegemonic narratives of asylum circulating within the rhetorical ecology of the U.S. asylum system?

My answers to each of these questions illustrate how meaningful advocacy efforts can be built through listening to shelter rhetorics because they draw attention to the wider networks in which asylum narratives are constructed.

How does LPP operate as a rhetorical network within the rhetorical ecology of the U.S. asylum system?

LPP operates as a Third Space by fostering shelter rhetorics and through its networked positioning within overlapping rhetorical ecologies of the U.S. asylum system and the Rio Grande Valley. In Chapter 3, I argued that spatial conventions of meaning-making impact how someone seeking asylum is understood and tolerated. I understand that as "asylum-seekers," the clients I spoke to bear labels that are associated with criminalization, emphasized within spaces like detention centers or airports. However, because LPP operates within the Rio Grande Valley, it also affords meaning-making based on shifting identities and transience. Thus, LPP's positioning within the RGV allows it to pull from *una cultura mestiza* (Anzaldúa 44) in order to afford clients an opportunity to name themselves on their own terms.

One important implication of this work, then, is how a blended rhetorical ecology methodology allowed me to trace the transnational rhetorics at the shelter. In Chapter 2, I described how I leaned on rhetorical ecology's argument that meaning is made through shifting, intertwined, located contexts that are formed through a variety of humans, non-humans, and sociopolitical conditions along with Chicana feminism's emphasis on the rhetorical possibility and agency of (dis)located and marginalized people within liminal spaces. Through that blend, I was inspired by *la mesa redonda*, a vibrant thing from the shelter's outdoor space that helped inform how this project is grounded in four axioms: materiality, equitability, permeability, and diversity.

Materiality helped me appreciate how the participant's meaning-making is bound in material positioning, beginning with physical bodies (including race, gender, sexuality, age, and (dis)ability) and extending out to geographical locations as well as sociopolitical climates. Equitability allowed me to trace the variety of human and non-human things in a rhetorical context that impacted participants' experiences and perspectives. Permeability helped me understand how participants' movement in the world jolts them into shifting and transformative rhetorical ecologies, affecting how they are able to make meaning within new contexts. The permeability of rhetorical networks can be arduous but also beneficial in that it highlights the plurality of identity. And diversity helped me pay attention to these plural identities and messy narratives which do not fit the hegemonic frames of the asylum experience in a neat and tidy way.

Located-listening, I explained, was formed within the shelter from my vantage point as a volunteer first and then a scholar, and this methodological approach is unique to this particular place. As a methodology, located-listening is important because as transnational rhetorical feminists will argue, marginalized people are often simply reduced to stereotypical narratives and representations, namely, as victims in the Global South in need of salvation by the Global North in the form of neoliberal interventions. According to Dingo in "Macro and Micro," "there is an absence of a structural critique so that we are unable to see or understand how transglocal [Dingo and Scott] power relationships are literally transferred onto women's bodies and lives" (532). In addition, Dingo explains that often "neoliberal rhetoric, then, obfuscates the wider contextual problems that constrain people's choices and their investments. Additionally, this neoliberal rhetoric allows people with money, presumably from wealthy countries, to separate themselves from those in whom they are investing" ("Macro and Micro," 533). In Networking Arguments, Dingo explains that "by turning to transnational feminist theory, feminist rhetoricians can learn how to network arguments so that they might gauge the various and shifting representational and material effects of globalization" on marginalized people (8). As Dingo explains, there is a need for "rhetoric and composition scholars to examine critically our own literacy, writing practices, and pedagogies making sure that we connect localized and individual micro-stories to global macro-conditions" (Dingo, "Macro and Micro," 536). I recommend researchers employ adapted versions of "located-listening" in their own unique work with displaced populations.

How does the shelter, as a networked site, afford or constrain the variety of stories people seeking asylum tell about their lived experiences?

This book focused on two shelter rhetorics: silence and routine. Both of these shelter rhetorics work to agentively protect (shelter) the person seeking asylum, either through concealment of their story or by sharing a new story about themselves; in this way, both silence and routine work toward resisting the mainstream narratives of victimization that overshadow displaced people's lives and also allow clients to name themselves.

Implications of Silence as a Shelter Rhetoric

It is important to notice how silence works at LPP because silence is one of many echoes of displacement that clients may use upon transitioning from their previous region's rhetorical ecology into their new rhetorical ecology of the U.S. asylum system. I have shown that people seeking asylum compose stories about their persecution and displacement in public and private contexts (Chapter 4). These contexts are difficult to navigate for people seeking asylum because they require storytellers to shift abruptly from narrative norms from their previous communities to norms in the U.S. which often require consistency, detail, and chronological tellings. Through participants' stories and visualizations, I described how, as part of a Third Space, the people at

LPP make room for clients to construct their own stories by first listening to clients' "echoes of displacement," or the stories which reflect traces of or reverberated responses to the trauma of persecution and dislocations of home. By listening to silences, the staff and clients offer rhetorical support to tell stories with dignity and welcome clients to share their stories on their own terms, not with the goal of domination (persuasion), but with the intent of mutual understanding. It was clear that folks who participated in this study understood how their position as rhetors, their message, and their audiences are in flux; as their bodies move, they enter varying rhetorical ecologies, each with their own histories, cultural rhetorical practices, and materiality. I understand that people seeking asylum require a Third Space, or a space which allows them to slowly and discursively construct their own spaces based on non-binary, often contradictory, and messy rhetorics. Third Spaces allow clients to tell stories on their own terms, in their own time, and for their own alternative purposes (Flores), and doing so is made possible by an environment which demonstrates a sensitivity to their silence as a rhetorical reverberation, or echo of their displacement.

One recommendation that I offer from this study, then, is fostering advocacy efforts that listen to echoes of displacement, like silences, in order to help clients tell their stories as connected to larger contexts and rhetorical ecologies. One such initiative that culminated from this project and attempts to promote transnational rhetorical literacies is a writing consultation program which partnered faculty and students from my teaching institution, the University of Texas Rio Grande Valley (UTRGV), as well as shelter clients and staff. This writing consultation program was built to cultivate rhetorics that trace the distributed agency of the credible fear people seeking asylum face, even within the U.S. asylum system itself (Reyes et al.).

This initiative was created at the end of Spring 2019 when I casually asked the campus writing center associate director, who is also an associate professor in the department, if he and the campus writing tutors would be able to help interested clients at LPP write about their experiences. After a summer of planning with LPP, the initiative now offers writing and/or translation (Spanish and French) services for interested clients to communicate their narrative about their asylum claims through one-to-one consultations. While clients would be able to take this narrative to legal counsel to continue their claim process, the faculty and shelter staff see this initiative more as providing "rhetorical listening" (Foss and Griffin) as well as resources for clients to be able to tell their story in a safe, nonjudgmental context. The initiative had no name at the outstart, so I nicknamed it "the mobile writing lab" because it mobilizes UTRGV faculty and students to the shelter space, and by composing their stories, people seeking asylum may be mobilized to gain opportunities associated with submitting a formal asylum application. Ultimately, we officially referred to the writing consultation program as *Rhetorica del Refugio* to reflect the spirit of shelter rhetorics in the space, and the consultations began in 2019 and slowly partnered with interested clients and faculty until the COVID-19 pandemic greatly limited and eventually halted the partnership.

While the mobile writing lab was spearheaded by the UTRGV writing center associate director and myself, we planned the initiative with the executive director, the client coordinator, the weekend coordinator (who was also a previous client and still lived on site), and a student-intern who had extensive paralegal experience. After three focus group meetings, my faculty colleague and I collaborated with these staff members (including the former client) to co-lead a training that took interested writing faculty through the complex maze of seeking asylum in the U.S. The training especially focused on how storytelling and writing a credible narrative is essential in making an asylum claim. Through the staff's expertise as well as my emerging analysis of data for this book, the faculty group learned about this process and how their own expertise with rhetoric and composition may help interested clients tell their stories in a direct and detailed way. In addition, the student-intern as well as a former client/(current) weekend coordinator both offered firsthand experience of the many struggles clients face in composing such credible fear narratives, and how a writing expert may help someone overcome such obstacles with sensitivity and patience.

We learned from staff how to ask important questions as clients shared their stories as well as how to pay attention to silences. These techniques helped faculty and willing clients collaborate to compose a story that contextualized the client's persecution and oppression. The faculty brought their scholarly expertise, but they also contributed their many combined years of teaching along the U.S.-Mexico border, experience with advocacy work, as well as Spanish and French skills.

Reflecting on this initiative, I understand some limitations that are important to discuss. For one, clients who choose to participate may experience (for obvious reasons) discrepancies of power between themselves and the faculty volunteers. In addition, while each visit takes roughly 2–3 hours in order to hear client's stories, ask questions, and help them articulate their experiences in writing in a clear way, these interactions do not mirror the conversations that Ayana describes which happen around *la mesa redonda* (Chapter 4). At *la mesa redonda*, the conversations occur daily among (somewhat) familiar faces; the conversations also contain opportunities for individuals to first listen to others' stories and choose silence. In other words, the mobile writing lab consultations are not organic conversations, despite their best intentions to be so and despite how forthcoming clients can be about their experiences and their gratitude for our help. What is more, the consultations may mirror the credible fear interview that clients have endured because of the nature of the conversation and the power differential between the faculty volunteer and the client. My colleagues and I didn't find a clear solution around this, as the clients who have participated are not long-term stays at the shelter, making more paced and steady connections and relationships an impossibility. I consider that initiatives like the mobile writing lab work best in concert with the organic "invitational rhetoric" (Foss and Griffin) practices already at work in spaces like LPP.

Despite these limitations, the efforts the faculty and clients make toward collaborative storytelling is one way to combat reductive portrayals of the asylum experience. The mobile writing lab is essentially advocating for more nuanced and meaningful representations of marginalization and oppression (Hesford, "Cosmopolitanism," 55). By asking questions about their home communities and the specific types of persecution and layers of oppression they faced, the faculty consultants and clients work together to put aside simplistic representations of displaced people and delve into the intricate networks and "political structures and processes, global economic systems, or colonial histories that imbricate systematic … violence against marginalized populations]" that are often neglected ("Macro and Micro" 532). In fact, as faculty spent more time at the shelter working with clients, they were able to observe firsthand how "Remain in Mexico" (Chapter 3) radically reduced populations at the shelter. We brainstormed about how we could work with people in detention who were making their way to LPP, but we learned how difficult communicating with incarcerated immigrants was. We were experiencing how meaning-making is "shaped by cultural, social, and economic interconnectivities and interrelations and cross-border and cross-cultural mobilizations of power, language and resources, and people" (Hesford and Schell 465). In other words, we experienced how policed borders, criminalization of immigrants (Chapter 3), and limited material resources inhibited us from connecting with people to help them tell their stories.

In the end, the faculty became involved in the rhetorical ecology of the U.S. asylum system through networking with LPP. Their assistance helped people compose stories they would use for asylum claims, and through staff and clients' expertise we learned displacement narratives are networked in problematic and complex ecologies, often working against conventions and narrative norms from clients' home regions.

Implications of Routine as a Shelter Rhetoric

In Chapter 5, I discussed the importance of routine for clients to compose new narratives that resist mainstream narratives centered on displaced people as victims. I specifically examined the routines of crocheting, housework, and singing to demonstrate how routine allows clients to enact agency through *rasquache* rhetorics (Medina-López) or daily practices that develop a "rhetoric of difference" about asylum experience (Flores). Through sharing routines with other clients, clients created narratives that fracture hegemonic perspectives of people seeking asylum. The specific narratives of resistance I observed at LPP were "I am useful"; "I have a family"; "and "I am patriotic without citizenship." Each of these narratives was told as clients assembled with material things and spaces at the shelter to help them compose new stories about themselves while being displaced. Such an observation demonstrates how significant routine is to make meaning, and this includes the quotidian objects and spaces that are often taken for granted in the lives of displaced people.

Listening to the alternative narratives that clients told about themselves is significant because it helps audiences understand the plurality of identity of people seeking asylum. If the previous initiative focused specifically on networked stories of persecution, I also see room for advocacy efforts which draw attention to the daily life or routines of people seeking asylum.

A first-year writing course I taught in the Spring of 2019 at UTRGV makes for an apt illustration of such a recommendation. The course focused on how forced migration is represented in various contexts and required students to engage in rhetorical ecology analysis of our own RGV as a place of importance for people seeking asylum; students also traced ecologies of narratives of displacement from media outlets. In addition to bi-monthly service visits to the shelter, our main contacts from LPP joined my students and me at the university four times during the semester, twice for in-person visits to share their expertise about asylum experience, once via webcam to join our class for a forced migration expert's invited talk about her work (Frydenlund), and once through a conference call to collaborate on outreach materials that my students were creating for the shelter. Such ongoing dialogue fostered community-engagement that highlighted how LPP and my students were each learning from each other; however, this interaction also brought both parts of this service-learning course into one another's routines. Through routine interactions, my students were able to begin listening to displacement narratives with a more contextual understanding of the larger rhetorical ecologies in which these narratives are told. In sum, I aimed to foster transnational literacies alongside my students through direct service at the shelter, rhetorical ecology analysis activities, and a collaborative public document assignment to promote the shelter's needs.

The course began with direct service to the shelter where my students served in a variety of roles: language tutors in the English language learning (ELL) classes, Spanish translators for client documents (as in the stories they would use on asylum applications), as well as outdoor maintenance workers alongside clients. Such responsibilities helped students participate in the shelter rhetoric of routine firsthand.

After each visit, students also wrote in their reflection journals (similar to field notes) about how the service was informing their course projects and perspective on the issue of migration in their own RGV community. As the students visited the shelter, they were able to find material ways to connect clients' lives and stories to larger systems of oppression that are often overlooked. For example, one student wrote in his reflection journal about the instinct he had to hear client stories on a more personal level while volunteering in the ELL classroom, and his curiosity revealed greater insight about the client's home:

> One of my main problems whenever I was helping is that I would stop teaching them for a bit and just connect with them and listen to their life stories and share a few of my own. It was nice to bond and share stories with the people there, although the sisters would always remind me to not stop teaching them English, I would often forget and continue getting off topic. But upon sharing stories I found out that one of the aslyum [sic] seekers at La Posada was born in the same town as my father!

This student was able to position the client's story more contextually by spending time with the client in a routine ELL class. Forming this "bond" through conversation and learning allowed both client and student to be vulnerable enough to share their own stories. What resulted was the student taking a greater interest in his own host community's role as a border space: "Before I took this English course, I just did not care about all the things happening at the border, or about talks about building the wall. But after experiencing what I have experience [sic] at La Posada, I feel a lot more passionate about anything border related."

Students also surveyed readings appropriate to the ecology and discipline through scaffolded scholarly reading and writing assignments that provided paced opportunities to analyze the rhetorical ecology of asylum narratives. Keeping first-year writing course learning outcomes in mind, the readings I chose that are about migration are essentially more about the rhetorics of migration; the text's rhetorical focus dovetailed with texts from Wardle and Downs' *Writing about Writing*. For example, we began the semester by having open discussions and private writing sessions about what we knew about asylum and "asylum-seekers." Students also read national and local news stories about the RGV as a site of international interest concerning asylum, and they critiqued the legitimacy of framing asylum as a "problem" or "crisis" in our area. For example, students read "Words That Work: Making the Best Case for People Seeking Asylum" by the Asylum Seeker Resource Centre, or the article "Why Does the Media Keep Showing Those Same Pictures? A Greek Host Community's Ongoing Struggle" by one of my planned guest speakers and colleagues (Frydenlund). Such readings provide arguments not simply about migration issues, but about the implications of how migration is represented in the media as a problem to be solved. For instance, Taylor's "Why the Language We Use to Talk about Refugees Matters So Much" argues that the labels that describe various migrants such as refugees or "asylum seekers" have unique and troubling connotations in certain places and contexts.

As students visited the shelter and participated in client's routines, they were able to build a transnational literacy that critiqued the implications of framing people seeking asylum as "problems." One student shared in her journal: "Seeing how people spoke about people seeking asylum before volunteering, I felt like they weren't being spoken about as people, but as a threat. Being able to talk to the clients at La Posada has reminded me that these are real people with stories that need to be heard."

Another student commented on the diversity of stories she heard and how the stories resist neat and tidy frameworks. The following excerpt is from a student who helped with gardening at the shelter alongside fellow clients:

> The crowd that was cutting the grass consisted of a man who is fractured from a hand, five women, and four children. As I cut the grass, I would talk to them basic stuff such as the weather and where I lived. They would be shy at first, but then they would tell me their situation and the cause of why they fled. Each situation was different, one was because of a jealous husband threatening the wife, and most of them fled because of their government and Insecurity ... They had to converse with various people in order to cross the Mexican border and into the United States. As they told their story, they would ask me questions such as "What would you do in that case?", or "Why do people do that, is it part of their culture?" I had no idea of what to answer because I have never placed myself in those types of situations. What they suffered and lived made me realize that there [are] bigger problems out there than what I think simple problems are.

By hearing stories and understanding the narrative journey that people seeking asylum face, this student was forming a literacy that does not allow her to reduce the client's experiences in a way that homogenizes their stories. In addition, she has no answer for clients who worked alongside her in the shelter yard when one asked her about the U.S. demand for narrative credibility about his persecution. At the very least, this student's grappling with how to account for such narrative standards of credibility positions her to ask deeper questions about the immigration policies that this client faces.

The course culminated in a collaborative "action research project" (Ingram et al.) of three separate public documents, each created by small student groups. These public documents (any genre that would address the public, such as a poster, flier, or webpage, for example) helped support the shelter's fundraising and awareness campaigns, but interestingly, my students each centralized the routines of the shelter in their public documents. For example, students created digital posters that called for volunteers to help lead exercise classes at the shelter, teach and care for children during the adult ELL classes, and create video content for the shelter's *YouTube* channel. Students and I discussed how the needs for exercise and language classes help foster a plurality of identity for shelter clients. Their humanity is highlighted by advocating for volunteers to nourish the needs many people share, like exercise to offset anxiety or childcare to have time to learn new skills. Most notably, these public documents were not simply calling for donations of things or money that often perpetuate both the victimization or tidy solution of "giving" that hovers over advocacy efforts within displacement contexts.

Because the assignment involved students making an argument that may be useful for LPP to build partnerships with the community, my students had to communicate with the shelter, especially their executive director and communications director, to understand LPP's needs and rhetorical goals as well as styles of argumentation. This project helped my students imagine LPP's audience and meaningfully contribute to the rhetorical ecology themselves while completing a semester of bi-monthly service visits.

Cooper argues that the kind of writing that my students did for the public document assignment plays a significant part in formulating, identifying, and sustaining ecology. She writes, "[w]riting is an activity through which a person is continually engaged with a variety of socially constituted systems," or their ecology (367). By focusing on the daily lives of people seeking asylum and their routines, my students presented a perspective of clients and displacement that would disturb the fixed-identity and stagnant messages of asylum experience in order to draw partners of advocacy to the shelter.

Additionally, this public document assignment also positioned my students to employ transnational rhetorical literacies in asylum contexts directly. Students had to account for their rhetorical choices and the implications of those choices in light of the rhetorical frames of victimization and loss that overshadow the asylum experience that they had read about in our course. My students grappled with the cost of forsaking victim narratives and employing more alternative rhetorics. They considered how people may not be inclined to give their time and energy to someone who didn't seem like a victim. These questions were difficult, and while there were no easy answers within a semester of a first-year writing course, my students were able to experience, through shared routines, how people seeking asylum contain a plurality of identities.

How do the stories produced at the shelter perpetuate or critique the hegemonic narratives of asylum circulating within the rhetorical ecology of the U.S. asylum system?

The stories produced at the shelter are messy in that they are difficult to classify as purely subversive or hegemonic; because LPP is positioned between two distinct rhetorical ecologies that operate with distinct conventions, the stories at the shelter contain traces of hegemonies and resistance. What such messy stories demonstrate is the transitory nature of the space. In other words, as a Third Space, LPP provides opportunities for marginalized people to cultivate alternative perspectives and shared rhetorical practices which speak back to hegemonic and fixed representations of their experiences. But this takes time, and clients exemplified a state of "becoming" or transition by enacting shelter rhetorics like silence and routines.

As I've noted previously, Third Space is not a site that advocates for an overtaking of one binary opposition of another; instead, those in a Third Space value plural and hybrid discourses, identities, and meanings forged by their own rhetorics of daily life. For example, in Chapter 5, a complex narrative I observed was "I am patriotic without citizenship." This narrative shows traces of resistance and hegemony as exemplified in Esther's routine of raising the U.S. flag to exercise patriotism to a country in which she is not a citizen. The straightforward and conventional way she demonstrates patriotism is obviously leaning on well-established discourses of what loyalty to a country looks like (singing patriotic songs, honoring symbols of the nation, like flags) in order to write herself into the rhetorical ecology of the U.S. asylum system in recognizable ways. At the same time, the fact that she is not a citizen makes this performance one of resistance. She is defying the norms of such acts by celebrating the nation as a person seeking asylum or a person in a state of transition, movement, and mobility, not necessarily toward citizenship, but toward a Third Space culture that is based on non-binary labels.

In Puumala and Pehkonen's study of people seeking asylum in Finland who had been given a decision similar to "withholding of removal," the authors also noted the "becoming" state of displaced people as they grapple with their precarity within "interzones," which are similar to Third Spaces: "The interzone is an opportunity for transformation, for 'the political' to take place and allow the body to articulate itself beyond asylum politics 'as usual'" (Puumala and Pehkonen 53). What is important is that the LPP clients are able to "identify themselves as different from dominant culture and thus are able to establish self- and/or group autonomy because they name themselves" (Zepeda 142). Esther's raising the flag, for example, draws a balanced attention both to her difference from the dominant culture (lack of citizenship) and her autonomy to participate in such a patriotic act despite her lack of citizenship. She becomes uncategorizable. Such routines should not be discounted in their efficacy to unite a community to (re)vision the hegemonic discourse surrounding them.

Building Bridges

I admit that it is difficult for me to consider research with displaced people who do not have goals for advocacy because that is how I was introduced to the complex lives of those seeking asylum in the first place. I understand that not all researchers who do work similar to this project see themselves as volunteers or activists first; however, like rhetorician Ellen Cushman, I think that research should have material effects on the lives of the people we write about ("Public Intellectual" 330). At a time when many in the U.S. are harshly divided on the issue of immigration, I sincerely wonder how gallery walks, exhibitions, or other traditional forms of research dissemination cut through the noise of the media's overwhelming coverage of asylum; there is no shortage of powerful photo stories or human-interest perspectives. Such works are vitally important; however, if they do not engage with audiences in ways that offer meaningful contexts for asylum experience, such works may do more harm than good if they reduce the problems and solutions of asylum in ways that perpetuate the problematic networks between the Global North and South. Instead, the initiatives which have manifested from this research motivate what Cushman calls "change at a micro level of interaction" ("Social Change" 14). It is through this more intimate layer of exchange, built on shelter rhetorics of silences and routines, that a deeper understanding of the complex issue of asylum may be able to emerge. And like Cushman, I understood that this scholarship would be effective if it could engage to "bridge the university and community through activism" ("Social Change" 7).

Indeed, I see this project and the advocacy outcomes as a bridge, as bridges convey connection, exchange, and a path for mobility. In addition to demonstrating how rhetoric is paramount in helping people seeking asylum bridge their way to safety, I've also taken the long path out to describe how transnational literacies are meaningful in tracing the variety of scaled connections and bridges which displaced people traverse to overcome oppression. Finally, this work may help more places like LPP simply and routinely treat displaced people with respect and dignity to collaboratively build the kinds of bridges necessary to lead less precarious lives (Figure 6.2).

Figure 6.2 Resources in the ELL classroom, including a whiteboard with the lyrics to the song "Love Can Build a Bridge" by The Judds. Photo by Michelle.

References

Anzaldúa, Gloria. *Borderlands/La Frontera: The New Mestiza*. Aunt Lute Books, 1987.

Asylum Seeker Resource Centre. "Words That Work: Making the Best Case for People Seeking Asylum." 5 Aug. 2018. https://www.asrc.org.au/wp-content/uploads/2016/05/ASRC-Words-that-Work-4pp.pdf. Accessed 12 Jan. 2019.

Cooper, Marilyn M. "The Ecology of Writing." *College English*, vol. 48, no. 4, 1986, pp. 364–75.

Cushman, Ellen. "The Public Intellectual, Service Learning, and Activist Research." *College English*, vol. 61, no. 3, 1999, pp. 328–36. *JSTOR*, https://www.jstor.org/stable/379072.

Cushman, Ellen. "The Rhetorician as an Agent of Social Change." *College Composition and Communication*, vol. 47, no. 1, 1996, pp. 7–28. *JSTOR*, http://www.jstor.org/stable/358271.

Dingo, Rebecca. "Networking the Macro and Micro: Toward Transnational Literacy Practices." *JAC*, vol. 33, no. 3/4, 2013, pp. 529–52.

Dingo, Rebecca. "Reevaluating Girls' Empowerment: Toward a Transnational Feminist Literacy." *Circulation, Writing & Rhetoric*, edited by Laurie Gries and Collin Gifford Brooke, Utah State UP, 2018, pp. 135–51.

Flores, Lisa A. "Creating Discursive Space through a Rhetoric of Difference: Chicana Feminists Craft a Homeland." *Quarterly Journal of Speech*, vol. 82, no. 2, 1996, pp. 142–56, *Routledge*.

Foss, Sonja K. and Cindy L. Griffin. "Beyond Persuasion: A Proposal for an Invitational Rhetoric." *Communication Monographs*, vol. 62, 1995, pp. 2–18, *EBSCO*.

Frydenlund, Erika. "Why Does the Media Keep Showing Those Same Pictures? A Greek Host Community's Ongoing Struggle." *The Migrationist*, 4 Jul. 2017. https://themigrationist.wordpress.com/2017/07/04/why-does-the-media-keep-showing-those-same-pictures-a-greek-host-communitys-ongoing-struggle/h. Accessed 12 Jan. 2019.

Hesford, Wendy S. "Cosmopolitanism and the Geopolitics of Feminist Rhetoric." *Rhetorica in Motion: Feminist Rhetorical Methods and Methodologies*, edited by Eileen E. Schell and K. J. Rawson, University of Pittsburgh Press, Pittsburgh, PA, 2010, pp. 53–70.

Hesford, Wendy S. and Eileen Schell. "Configurations of Transnationality: Locating Feminist Rhetorics." *College English*, vol. 70, no. 5, 2008, pp. 461–70. *JSTOR*, http://www.jstor.org/stable/25472283.

Ingram, Maia, et al. "Community Engagement Strategies in a Participatory Action Research Study with Farmworkers." *Handbook of Social Inclusion*. Springer International Publishing, pp. 1505–24, https://doi.org/10.1007/978-3-030-89594-5_82.

Medina-López, Kelly. "Rasquache Rhetorics: A Cultural Rhetorics Sensibility." *Constellations*, vol. 1, no. 1, 2018. http://constell8cr.com/issue-1/rasquache-rhetorics-a-cultural-rhetorics-sensibility/.

Puumala, Eeva and Samu Pehkonen. "Corporeal Choreographies between Politics and the Political: Failed Asylum Seekers Moving from Body Politics to Bodyspaces." *International Political Sociology*, vol. 4, 2010, pp. 50–65.

Royster, Jacqueline Jones. *Traces of a Stream: Literacy and Social Change among African American Women*. University of Pittsburgh Press, 2000.

Smith, Linda Tuhiwai. *Decolonizing Methodologies: Research and Indigenous Peoples*. 2nd ed., Zed Books, 1999.

Powell, Malea. "Listening to Ghosts a (non)Argument." *ALT DIS: Alternatives to Academic Discourse*, edited by Helen Fox and Christopher Schroeder, Cook-Heinemann, 2002, pp. 11–22.

Reyes, Monica, et al. "Enacting Invitational Rhetorics: Leveraging Networks of Care in the U.S. Asylum Process." *Grassroots Activisms: Public Rhetorics in Localized Contexts*, edited by Lisa L. Phillips et al., Ohio State UP, 2024, pp. 235–50.

Riley-Mukavetz, Andrea M. "Towards a Cultural Rhetorics Methodology: Making Research Matter with Multi-generational Women from the Little Traverse Bay Band." *Rhetoric, Professional Communication and Globalization*, vol. 5, no. 1, 2014, pp. 108–25.

Taylor, Adam. "Why The language We Use to Talk About Refugees Matters So Much." *The Washington Post*, 30 July 2015, https://www.washingtonpost.com/news/worldviews/wp/2015/07/30/why-the-language-we-use-to-talk-about-refugees-matters-so-much/h. Accessed 12 Jan. 2019.

Wardle, Elizabeth and Doug Downs, editors. *Writing about Writing: A College Reader*. Bedford/St. Martin's, 2016.

Zepeda, Candace. "Chicana Feminism." *Decolonizing Rhetoric & Composition Studies*, edited by Iris D. Ruiz and Raul Sánchez, Palgrave Macmillan, 2016, pp. 137–51.

Appendix

Appendix A

Interview Questions

Preliminary Interview Prompt (Client Participants):

- Tell me, in any way that is most comfortable to you, about your journey to the U.S.
- Tell me about how you got to LPP.
  - Describe a typical day for you at LPP. Tell me where you spend your time here.
  - Who has been helpful here at LPP as you go through your asylum application process, especially with writing your story as part of your application?

Visualization Prompt:

- *Sketch Option:* In any way that is most comfortable to you, with any images or words you choose, I would like you to draw a picture of LPP on the paper provided. Make sure to include the most important spaces and areas at or around the shelter where you experience the freedom to talk, receive or ask for help in your asylum process, and plan for your future.
- *Photovoice Option:* I would like you to take some photos of LPP with the camera provided. During the next two days, take as many photos as you would like, but when you are done, choose your favorite ten photos that show the most important spaces and areas at or around the shelter where you experience the freedom to talk, receive or ask for help in your asylum process, and plan for your future. Then, on a separate paper, I would like you to write a sentence or two for each of those ten photos describing the photo and why you took it.
  - To protect other residents, make sure not to photograph anyone's face.

Follow-up:

- Please share your drawing/photos with me. Tell me about what you created.
- What areas or things have been helpful here at LPP as you go through your asylum application process, especially with writing your story as part of your application?
- What is/was particularly challenging or stressful about preparing your asylum application while at LPP?
- Do you ever share your story with others or hear others' stories here? If so, what is/was particularly helpful about these instances of telling your story?
- Did you learn anything about *how* to tell your story in these instances?

(Staff Participants)

- Describe how you began working with LPP.
- What is your role at the shelter?
- What is a typical day for you here at LPP like?
- Do residents ever ask you for help with their asylum applications? Explain. How do you help them?
- What or who do you think would be helpful for residents to have access to here at LPP that could help them complete their applications?
- What are some resident success stories that you might share with others who are in the process of seeking asylum?

Appendix B

LPP Monday–Friday Schedule

8:00–9:00 am: Breakfast
9:30–11:30 am: English Language Learning
12:00–1:00 pm: Lunch
1:30–3:30 pm: English Language Learning
4:00–6:00 pm: Rest
6:00 pm: Dinner
7:00–9:00 pm: Shower/Language Tutoring/Free-Time
10:00 pm: Curfew

Index

Note: Page numbers in *italics* refer to figures.

www.ingramcontent.com/pod-product-compliance
Lightning Source LLC
LaVergne TN
LVHW010927110826
845149LV00013B/2508

* 9 7 8 1 0 3 2 3 9 4 3 0 5 *